GALATIANS

THE NEW TESTAMENT DISCOURSE ANALYSIS COMMENTARIES SERIES

New Testament Discourse Analysis Commentaries (NTDAC) is a new and innovative commentary series on the Greek text of the New Testament. The volumes in the series pay close attention to the New Testament books as individual texts, based upon an explicit discourse analytic model articulated in the commentary and exemplified in the linguistic analysis.

Discourse analysis is an already proven productive method of textual interpretation for New Testament studies. It implies a theory of linguistic description that encompasses the smaller parts of language, such as words and even morphemes, but focuses upon the higher levels, such as the clause, the paragraph, and entire text as a meaningful unit. Discourse analysis—which may have a bottom-up or a top-down approach, or both—is not limited by traditional grammar but analyzes such linguistic features as the information structure, ideas and actions, and participant relations of a text, among other concerns. The interpretation provides both specific commentary supporting larger linguistic observations and broader commentary instantiated in textual particulars. The result is functional commentary useful to scholars for detailed knowledge of the Greek text and to practitioners for textually based information for preaching and teaching.

In the current landscape of commentary writing, in which commentaries have too often become simply comments on other commentaries, the NTDAC stands out by offering something different, compelling, and challenging. This is not to say that previous scholarship and reception history are irrelevant, but rather that the priority in the NTDAC is first and foremost a discourse analysis of the Greek text. In many ways, the series marks a return to what New Testament commentaries were originally designed to do, explicate the Greek text. However, the series seeks to do much more than that by introducing new observations on the Greek text that push interpretive boundaries and support previous findings by providing new linguistic insights.

The contributors to NTDAC approach the Greek text from a range of linguistic backgrounds. Nevertheless, they hold in common their desire to provide fresh interpretations of each book of the New Testament, based upon a specific discourse method.

STANLEY E. PORTER
MCMASTER DIVINITY COLLEGE
HAMILTON, ON, CANADA

GALATIANS

A Discourse Commentary

RANDALL K. J. TAN

◦PICKWICK *Publications* • Eugene, Oregon

GALATIANS
A Discourse Commentary

Copyright © 2025 Randall K. J. Tan. All rights reserved. Except for brief quotations in critical publications or reviews, no part of this book may be reproduced in any manner without prior written permission from the publisher. Write: Permissions, Wipf and Stock Publishers, 199 W. 8th Ave., Suite 3, Eugene, OR 97401.

Pickwick Publications
An Imprint of Wipf and Stock Publishers
199 W. 8th Ave., Suite 3
Eugene, OR 97401

www.wipfandstock.com

PAPERBACK ISBN: 978-1-5326-8561-3
HARDCOVER ISBN: 978-1-5326-8562-0
EBOOK ISBN: 978-1-5326-8563-7

Cataloguing-in-Publication data:

Names: Tan, Randall K. J. [author].

Title: Galatians : a discourse commentary / by Randall K. J. Tan.

Description: Eugene, OR: Pickwick Publications, 2025 | Series: New Testament Discourse Analysis Commentaries | Includes bibliographical references.

Identifiers: ISBN 978-1-5326-8561-3 (paperback) | ISBN 978-1-5326-8562-0 (hardcover) | ISBN 978-1-5326-8563-7 (ebook)

Subjects: LCSH: Bible.—Galatians—Commentaries. | Commentaries. | Greek language, Biblical—Discourse analysis. | Bible.—New Testament—Language, style.

Classification: BS2685.53 T36 2025 (paperback) | BS2685.53 (ebook)

12/09/25

CONTENTS

Preface | vii

INTRODUCTION TO THE LETTER TO THE GALATIANS

I. Foundational Assumptions | 1

II. Discourse Analysis | 5

COMMENTARY ON GALATIANS

1:1–5	**I. Letter Opening**	25
1:1–2	A. Setting the scene	26
1:3–5	B. Grace and peace come from Jesus rescuing us from the present evil age	34
1:6—2:21	**II. First Round of Rebuke, Backed by Extended Support**	37
1:6–9	A. Rebuke and changing perceptions	39
1:6–7	1. Undermining the "other gospel"	40
1:8–9	2. Curse pronouncement	44
1:10—2:21	B. Paul is a servant of Christ and proclaims a divine rather than human gospel	46
1:10	1. Transition to support: serving Christ as justification for opposing false gospel	47
1:11–12	2. Supporting premises: Paul proclaims a divine rather than human gospel	49

1:13—2:21	3. Supporting evidence from Paul's life and ministry | 50
3:1—4:7	**III. Second Round of Rebuke, Backed by Extended Support** | 68
3:1-6	A. Double-layered rebuke | 70
3:7—4:7	B. Only those who rely on faith are Abraham's true heirs | 73
3:7-14	1. Only those who rely on faith are blessed together with believing Abraham | 74
3:15—4:7	2. The inheritance does not rely on law, but rather on a promise | 77
4:8-31	**IV. Third Round of Rebuke** | 87
4:8-11	A. It is inconceivable for the Galatians to return to weak and poor elements | 89
4:12-20	B. Become like Paul, just as Paul had become like the Galatian Christians | 91
4:21-31	C. Call to listen to the law and recognize that they are children of the free woman, children of promise like Isaac | 95
5:1—6:10	**V. Extended Exhortation with Fourth Round of Rebuke Embedded** | 99
5:1-15	A. Stand firm in freedom, and do not be subject again to slavery | 101
5:16-26	B. Walk in the Spirit, and you will not carry out the desire of the flesh | 110
6:1-10	C. Let us work what is good for all, while we have the opportunity | 115
6:11-18	**VI. Letter Closing** | 121
6:11-17	A. Parting contrast between Paul and the opponents | 122
6:18	B. Closing benediction | 128

Bibliography \| 129

Modern Author Index \| 133

Scripture Index \| 135

PREFACE

This commentary offers a fresh discourse analysis of Paul's Letter to the Galatians. With a singular focus on the text, it is designed to help you comprehend Paul's message. We will ask what Paul is trying to do at each point by examining what he wrote and how he wrote it. At the same time, we will pay close attention to how form relates to function and how function relates to the situation. This is because what Paul said and how he said it reflect the social function he meant to accomplish.

You are invited to be my dialogue partner as we read Galatians together. You are encouraged to read this commentary with the Greek text of Galatians in front of you, where possible.[1] I will guide you through the questions I ask and explain the connections I make. Together, we will trace the discourse flow from one paragraph to the next and explore how different larger sections are connected. This interactive approach to analyzing Galatians will demonstrate how the various discourse elements harmoniously contribute to the whole, providing you with a holistic understanding.

Since my seminary days, I have felt the need for discourse commentaries for every book of the Bible. I am grateful to the series editor, Stan Porter, for inviting me to contribute this volume on Galatians. Stan's insightful comments on my initial draft were invaluable in refining the manuscript for publication. The fault for any remaining flaws and inadequacies is purely my own.

I would like to recognize my friends and former colleagues (at both Clear Bible, Inc. and Biblica), some of whom I have known for up to two

---

1. Besides this commentary, I would recommend Runge, *Discourse New Testament*, as a reading help. This resource annotates discourse features and includes an English interlinear gloss, morphology information, and links to specific entries in L&N for each Greek word. This kind of information and more can also be accessed at Symphony Browser. This is just a prototype interface to help you interact with the text, with lexical, morphological, syntactic, and discourse features assistance. Its link in the bibliography might change in the future.

decades: Rick Brannan, Steve Runge, Jonathan Robie, Sean Boisen, James Tauber, Ryder Wishart, Mike Brinker, Jake Wegner, James Cuénod, and Robertson Brinker. Working closely with them in recent years has been a privilege. May the Lord bless our efforts as we strive to develop the technology and digital resources necessary to give translators and the global church equal opportunity and ability to understand, obey, and teach the Scriptures.

Since the day I read through the entire New Testament in the NIV translation and came to faith, I have been on a continuous journey to deepen my understanding of the Bible. Before I gained sufficient proficiency in Greek, Hebrew, and Aramaic to read the Scriptures in their original languages almost exclusively, I learned much from reading through the whole Bible in the English NIV, NKJV, and NASB versions. Throughout this journey, I have been blessed by the support and influence of friends from Cru at the University of Kentucky, professors and fellow students at Southern Seminary, colleagues and students at Kentucky Christian University, various professional peers, and the different church communities I have been privileged to be a part of. I am grateful to the Lord for all the above.

My Greek and Hebrew professors at Southern Seminary—especially Tom Schreiner, Mark Seifrid, Peter Gentry, and Russell Fuller—instilled in me a deep love for the original languages and inspired me to dedicate my life to studying the Greek, Hebrew, and Aramaic Scriptures. Tom, my doctoral mentor, profoundly shaped how I analyze grammar and trace discourse flow in the Pauline Epistles.

During my doctoral research, I encountered the work of Stan Porter and Matt O'Donnell, with whom I had the privilege of collaborating on the OpenText.org project, annotating the entire Greek New Testament. The impact of Stan and Matt on my scholarly approach is immense.

I also extend my gratitude to my former employer, Clear Bible, Inc. (previously known as Global Bible Initiative and initially as Asia Bible Society), for assigning my esteemed former colleague, Andi Wu, and me to build digital corpora analyzing the Greek New Testament and the Hebrew Bible over many years. Along this journey, I gained valuable insights from many colleagues in biblical studies, Bible translation, and Bible technology. Steve Runge deserves special mention for deeply influencing how I analyze discourse.

I dedicate this volume to my family: my wife of over twenty years, Kimberly; our young children, Ruth, Matthew, and Hannah; my parents, Tony and Tammy; and my little sister Ranee. I would never have completed this volume without your sacrifices and encouragement. Each of you means the world to me. May I never take your steadfast love and support for granted!

Randall K. J. Tan
April 25, 2025

INTRODUCTION

This commentary is intentionally concise to make it easier for you to digest the analysis of Galatians as a whole. This introductory chapter will not cover traditional introductory issues to avoid potential duplication. Instead, we will address critical roles like author, recipients, and opponents in the relevant sections of the text, especially the letter opening (1:1–5) and occasion (1:6–9). While introductory background material and systematic overviews can often be helpful, they can also hinder you from reading the text with fresh eyes. Instead, we will focus on reading through the letter of Galatians together in sequence, focusing on what the text says, how it says it, and where it says it. We will intentionally limit how many preexisting assumptions we bring to the text and how often we jump ahead of the text. As much as possible, we will limit our reliance on background knowledge to what Paul seems to assume. When Paul does develop a theme within Galatians further, we will strongly privilege what Paul explicitly says in Galatians and limit our appeal to other scriptural passages that might be related. We will jump ahead in the text only when tracing how Paul develops a theme or portrays a participant throughout Galatians is helpful.

I. FOUNDATIONAL ASSUMPTIONS

While you can use the rest of the commentary without first reading this chapter, I will explain my foundational assumptions and method here to give you a fuller appreciation of my approach. That way, you will be better equipped to apply or adapt things as you see fit when you analyze other texts.

The New Testament texts are our primary source of information about the beliefs and practices of the early apostolic church after Jesus's resurrection. Moreover, much of what we know about the first century CE's language, culture, and history is also embedded within these same texts. Ideally, we would want to have native speakers of Hellenistic Greek interpret these texts for us. However, no one alive today is a native speaker. No scholar or interpreter (however well trained) is as familiar with the language of the New Testament as a native speaker. As a result, we must carefully analyze these texts individually and as a whole to understand the language, situation, and intended message.[1] Hence, this commentary will focus on the text of Paul's Letter to the Galatians rather than the secondary scholarly literature.[2] Specifically, I will apply an explicit linguistic method to make clear the structure, flow of ideas, and interaction of participants in the text.

How does linguistics help? We have to get past at least two hurdles. First, modern linguistics uses vocabulary and concepts quite different from those traditionally applied in biblical studies. Second, advocates of integrating modern linguistics into biblical studies draw from diverse theories and often use linguistic terminology differently. To keep the task more manageable, I will deliberately refrain from any deep exploration into linguistic theories here. Instead, I will only emphasize the aspects of modern linguistics that seem most relevant to the task. The following three general recommendations and their practical implications set the stage for my general approach.[3]

A. Multi-Angled, Multidisciplinary Approach

First, language is multifaceted. It is a tool for communicating and interacting with the world that cannot be reduced to an equation that can be neatly solved. For example, language can at least be viewed as a social fact, a psychological state, a set of structures, or a collection of outputs.[4] No theory comprehensively describes every aspect of language. Linguistic models reflect the perspectives and intentions of the people who originated them.

---

1. As Porter and O'Donnell contend, the most important question is how to study the text because the main evidence we have is the New Testament text and we have to do text-based study primarily (*Discourse Analysis*, 515).

2. One area where I will cite the secondary literature more than usual is in this chapter on theory and method. This is because my thinking on linguistic theory and method has definitely been shaped by others, which would be useful to make explicit. The second area is on textual variants (though I will skip some inconsequential variants others mention). This is because determining the best reading of the text of Galatians is foundational to focusing on the text of Paul's letter. Yet, at the same time, the text of Galatians is well attested, with few textual variants of significance. The uncertain cases tend to be of little interpretive significance. The secondary literature adequately addresses these variants. So, referencing them reduces the need for me to add my own independent treatment.

3. I have expressed these three general recommendations in an earlier form in Tan, "Linguistics and Biblical Studies."

4. Bauer, *Linguistics Student's Handbook*, 3.

They often aim to tackle specific concerns.[5] Consequently, different theories potentially contribute valuable insights from various perspectives.[6] Given this fact, I suggest approaching the analysis of texts from multiple angles. The main cautions to applying an eclectic method are:

1. To always keep in mind how different approaches fit within one's overall view of how language works
2. To apply them in a principled rather than ad hoc manner[7]

In addition, even though this commentary will consciously avoid becoming a commentary on other commentaries, previous scholarship will continue to serve as dialogue partners in my background research.[8] These dialogue partners bring different perspectives. Sometimes, they revealed gaps or blind spots in my analysis. Sometimes, at least one provided partial independent confirmation of a less common interpretive option. Frequently, interpreters come to similar or complementary conclusions about the text's message. This result is not surprising. In the end, we are all trying to interpret the same text. While linguistics provides a sound framework for analyzing the text, it need not yield new insights or overturn traditional interpretations.[9] Where there are real differences, the ultimate arbiter is how well our disparate interpretations account for the forest and the trees in the discourse of Galatians.

B. Caution and Restraint in Claims

Second, as much as possible, we should go only as far as the textual evidence allows.[10] In theory, different language levels can be analyzed separately.

5. Simpson, "Introduction: Applied Linguistics," 6.

6. As Porter and O'Donnell note, those engaged in discourse analysis recognize that "meaning in text is multilayered and may be approached in different ways" (*Discourse Analysis*, 63). Porter observed elsewhere that discourse analysis requires multidisciplinary study as it analyzes larger structures involving how words, participants, topics, and interpersonal, situational, and cultural contexts are weaved together (*Linguistic Analysis*, s.vv. "A Multidisciplinary Approach to Exegesis").

7. Porter and O'Donnell caution that one's procedure is compromised without a solid theory as a foundation (*Discourse Analysis*, 86–87).

8. I applied my discourse method on the Greek text and drafted my preliminary conclusions before consulting the secondary literature, including commentaries. Existing scholarship helped me evaluate, support, and refine my own work.

9. Porter, *Linguistic Analysis*, 92.

10. The process of understanding a text is often not straightforward. I went back and forth between top-down and bottom-up steps in conversation with the text, continually spiraling toward better understanding.

In practice, making fine-grained distinctions with text in context can be challenging. This is because attempts to make such distinctions can often go beyond the available textual evidence. Moreover, dividing the respective contributions of syntax and semantics can be problematic in language analysis.[11] Therefore, we must practice caution and restraint when claiming comprehensiveness and certainty for our analyses. If we follow this practice, we will equip ourselves to make well-founded claims. At the same time, we will position ourselves to help others exercise similar restraint and caution in their claims.

C. Language in Context

Third, the meaning of any text in context is simultaneously more and less than the sum of its parts when taken out of context. In the abstract, linguistic forms are generally under-specified, with a range of potential meanings. This is why words or phrases can mean different things when looked at by themselves. However, how words and phrases are used together with other words and phrases in a sentence or a larger discourse constrains their meaning.[12] This is because people who communicate know what they want to say and make appropriate choices to express their meaning.[13] These choices are reflected within the discourse itself, which we must interpret. Failure to recognize this fact can lead to various linguistic mistakes.[14] Therefore, we must pay systematic attention to contextual information within the text to accurately disambiguate the meaning of any linguistic utterance.

While I am generally happy to interpret Scripture with other parts of Scripture when necessary, I prioritize interpreting individual texts with other parts of itself when possible.[15] This is particularly important when

11. Some see the lexicogrammar of language as a continuum of paradigmatic systems, with grammar at one end and lexis at the other. See, e.g., Hasan, "Grammarian's Dream"; Hasselgård et al., *Corpus Perspectives*.

12. Greaves and Warren, "Multi-Word Units?," 212–26; Granger and Meunier, *Phraseology*; and Herbst et al., *Phraseological View of Language*.

13. Callow, *Man and Message* 2.2, "An Alternative Approach: Meanings Prior to Words."

14. Barr, *Semantics of Biblical Language*. These include "illegitimate totality transfer," "illegitimate identity transfer," and confusing lexical items with the concepts they may represent.

15. I assume that what Beekman and Callow assert about implicit information is true also more generally of most information needed to understand the message of a New Testament epistle like Galatians: "Most of the implicit information that is relevant to understanding the document is contained within the document itself, and it is only rarely necessary for the translator to draw on information from outside of it"

interpreting Paul's epistles because we have multiple letters from Paul, many of which share similar themes. My reasoning is as follows: When an author's message in a particular work is relatively clear and complete, it is unnecessary to introduce considerations from his or her other writings. After all, different works by the same author are written for different purposes and may communicate different messages, even when they share themes. Indeed, it can be counterproductive to let an author's other writings potentially overwhelm the distinctive message of a particular book. If he or she is indeed writing something different, that difference may become obscured or drowned out.

In addition, given that Paul has to rebuke and correct his audience throughout Galatians, he often has to communicate relatively clearly and elaborate more thoroughly than usual. So, I will particularly emphasize interpreting Galatians with Galatians in this commentary. In other words, I will prioritize interpreting the less clear parts of the letter with fuller explanations elsewhere in the letter. This practice aligns with my recommendations to exercise caution and restraint and interpret the text in context.[16]

II. DISCOURSE ANALYSIS

This commentary draws on functional linguistic theories like M. A. K. Halliday's systemic functional linguistics (SFL) and cross-linguistic, function-based analysis represented in Steven Runge's and Stephen H. Levinsohn's work. Functional theories and SFL provide the basic framework for understanding how language works. Attention to discourse features (such as what Runge and Levinsohn advocate) offers practical tools for bottom-up analysis of discourse flow. I will also draw relevant insights from epistolary studies on Paul's cultural context (especially on conventional expectations of letter structure).[17] Together, these provide the overall framework and

---

(*Translating Word of God*, 48). Unless otherwise specified, when appealing to context, I always mean the text surrounding the text in question. Some call this the context of text or co-text to distinguish it from the context of culture and the context of situation.

16. There are times when the text is relatively obscure. In such situations, we have to make guesses based on possible correspondence to clearer passages in Paul's other writings or even other parts of Scripture. When we do this, we have to be clear that we are making a guess. We know only that the meaning we derived is consistent with the other clearer passage(s) to which we appealed. However, we do not know with any certainty whether we have discerned Paul's intent in the obscure passage itself.

17. Epistolary studies has (1) demonstrated that Paul's letters should be treated as genuine letters; and (2) shed light on the opening, thanksgiving, and closing of Paul's letters as well as certain forms and transition formula used in ancient letters. See Jervis, *Purpose of Romans*; Reed, *Discourse Analysis of Philippians*, 153–295.

specific features I use to trace the flow of Paul's message. In addition, I draw on three related streams from biblical studies, Bible translation, and linguistics to track discourse flow.[18]

In practice, I analyzed the Greek text of Galatians and drafted my preliminary conclusions before returning to explain what assumptions and methods I used. So, this chapter was the last to be finalized. Meanwhile, Stan Porter and Matt O'Donnell, who were profoundly influential in forming my views on linguistics over two decades ago, published their long-awaited discourse analysis volume.[19] Happily, I discovered that they have provided well-researched and maturely thought-out support for many of the views we share. So, I will draw heavily from their work unapologetically to support this commentary's theoretical underpinnings and method below.

A. Explaining the Theory

SFL offers a comprehensive framework for analyzing texts by examining how language functions to create meaning in specific contexts. It recognizes that language has different levels and functions. On one level, to express yourself in writing, you start with the sounds and written symbols of the language. Next, the meaning, words, and grammar represent the content. This content, in turn, serves the social function appropriate for the situation and culture.[20] On another level, the overall text and its paragraphs, sentences (i.e., complex clauses), clauses, phrases (i.e., word groups), and words form a hierarchy. The larger units are made up of one or more units from the rank below it. For example, a clause comprises word groups that serve different syntactical functions within the clause. A word group is made up of words.[21]

---

18. I also remain deeply influenced by what my doctoral mentor, Tom Schreiner, calls tracing the argument (see Schreiner, *Interpreting the Pauline Epistles*). Kirk, "New Testament Argument Diagramming," traces the family tree of this technique (which is rooted in what Daniel Fuller called arcing) and shows how it is connected to related methods. I also find affinity with the analysis of semantic structure presented by Beekman and Callow, *Translating Word of God*, chs. 17–20. What I currently practice is closer to an enhanced form of rhetorical structure theory (RST). See Zeldes et al. "eRST," for a similar expansion of RST (but more geared towards computational discourse analysis). On the original expression of RST, see Mann and Thompson, *Theory of Text Organization*; or their condensed article "Rhetorical Structure Theory." It is notable that Fuller apparently influenced Beekman (Kirk, "New Testament Argument Diagramming," 11–12) while Mann and Thompson, in turn, acknowledged Beekman's influence on their work (Mann and Thompson, *Theory of Text Organization*, 38).

19. See Porter and O'Donnell, *Discourse Analysis*.

20. Halliday, *Introduction to Functional Grammar*, 24–27.

21. Halliday, *Introduction to Functional Grammar*, 5–10; Porter and O'Donnell, *Discourse Analysis*, 42.

In addition, some functions cut across different levels of language. When we communicate, we simultaneously:

1. Represent some content (ideational)
2. Interact with others (interpersonal)
3. Organize our message (textual)

These three metafunctions refer to the three main ways language creates meaning simultaneously in any communication.[22]

The ideational metafunction refers to how language construes experience and logical relationships. It represents the "content," i.e., what is being talked about.[23] The key to understanding what is happening at the ideational level is to examine how language represents ideas and experiences about the world.[24] A good place to begin is to analyze how the discourse depicts processes, participants, and circumstances from the bottom up. The combination of words and grammar conveys more than isolated meanings or ideas. It builds up a story within a world, whether real or imaginary.[25] The story includes characters who play various roles, different processes, and circumstances. You can consider the participants to be significant characters representing the entities (i.e., the who or what) most involved in the processes (i.e., what is happening) in the storyline. The processes are the happenings or states of affairs represented. They typically depict the actions the participants take and the events they experience. The circumstances are additional, usually optional, information about when, where, how, why, etc. involved in the process.[26]

The interpersonal metafunction refers to how language enacts social relationships. It includes things like the speaker's attitude and how the speaker relates to the audience.[27] The key to understanding what is happening in a text at an interpersonal level is to explore how language establishes

---

22. Porter and O'Donnell, *Discourse Analysis*, 11.

23. Halliday, *Introduction to Functional Grammar*, 30.

24. This is cross-linguistic, i.e., true of all languages. They are diverse in terms of how specifically they accomplish a task. However, every language has ways to accomplish basic tasks like depict the characters and circumstances involved, who is doing what to whom, and how events relate to one another. See Runge, *Discourse Grammar*, 6–7. See also Porter and O'Donnell, *Discourse Analysis*, 181–82.

25. Halliday: "'Architecture' of Human Language," 15–16; "Language Structure and Function," 143. Here I am using "story" in a broader sense than narrative, as representing the world in some way.

26. In Greek, the circumstances are frequently represented by prepositional phrases and adverbs.

27. Halliday, *Introduction to Functional Grammar*, 30.

and maintains social relationships between people. Typically, you start by analyzing things like mood, modality, and appraisal. With mood, we might ask if the speaker is making a statement, asking a question, or giving a command. With modality, the question involves the degree of certainty, obligation, or inclination expressed. With appraisal, we are concerned with how the speaker voices attitudes, judgments, and emotions. Viewed from a slightly different angle, besides understanding what content is depicted (ideational), we need to know if the speaker is exchanging information with the audience, trying to effect change, or sharing emotions and attitudes.[28]

The textual metafunction refers to how language organizes information to create a coherent message. The key is to explore how information is structured and flows in the discourse to create a unified whole.[29] This typically includes examining cohesion devices and how information flows and is highlighted within the flow. For example, connective words (usually conjunctions) frequently explicitly signal intended connections between clauses. In addition, it is generally helpful to look out for repeated use of the same lexical word or related words, including groups of words or clauses. Sometimes, the same words or words that share the same root are used to signal connections. Other times, related words, phrases, and clauses indicate related concepts and tie different paragraphs together.[30] It is necessary to watch out for these features while moving back and forth between the local context and the larger contexts of the overall text. This is especially vital to figure out how the parts relate to one another and the larger whole.

By applying this multilayered approach, SFL provides a comprehensive understanding of how a text creates meaning through language choices at various levels, from individual words to overall textual organization, all within the context of its social function. This understanding of language usage leads to the conclusion that comprehending the overall scene depicted by the text is just as important as interpreting it word by word. Furthermore, it is just as essential to explore how language functions and how that function relates to the situation as it is to analyze the actual form of the words

---

28. These are the three main purposes of human communication suggested by Callow (*Man and Message*, ch. 7).

29. Halliday speaks of "build[ing] up sequences of discourse, organizing the discursive flow, and creating cohesion and continuity as it moves along" (*Introduction to Functional Grammar*, 30). Porter and O'Donnell talk about "how the text is organized, how it coheres, and how it presents its information" (*Discourse Analysis*, 11).

30. On this kind of semantic field analysis, see, e.g., Halliday, "Language Structure and Function," 160. Porter and O'Donnell have a helpful chapter on cohesion and coherence (*Discourse Analysis*, 403–55).

used.[31] At the same time, the lexicogrammar and semantics of a text embody and present all these networks of choices made about meaning. Therefore, paying close attention to the lexicogrammar provides the foundation for bottom-up text analysis. Concurrently, exploration of semantics above the clause level proceeds from the other direction from the top down.[32]

1. Language as Context

My heavy emphasis on the text is founded on my understanding of how the text relates to the situation, culture, and language as a whole. This is a related but distinct point from what I explained in the Language in Context section above. In SFL, a specific text is an instance of the language as a system. At the same time, a particular situation is an instance of the overall culture. A text represents a specific situation, while the language system represents the overall culture.[33] This connection from culture and language to situation and text makes interpretation possible in the first place.

One might argue that most people implicitly operate under these assumptions when they study ancient languages or cultures through specific texts. However, caution and restraint are necessary since our primary access to the language, culture, and particular situations comes from Greek New Testament texts. Studying common structures in the many texts from a culture sheds light on typical genres in that culture. Comparing and contrasting with common structures in these genres can, in turn, provide helpful insights into a specific text. However, genre is more a guide than a determinative framework.

2. Genres and Subgenres

Genres follow socially agreed-upon conventions developed over time. Stories seem to be universal across cultures and time. So, one broad "universal"

---

31. Reed, *Discourse Analysis of Philippians*, 37. As Porter and O'Donnell note, all functional theories see language as a "tool for communication and social interaction." Language is in "a reciprocal relationship with its setting or context" (*Discourse Analysis*, 62). In turn, text is "the product of a linguistic act and reflects the process of continuous semantic choice with the result being that the text is a form of social exchange of meanings" (162).

32. See Porter and O'Donnell, *Discourse Analysis*, 33–34.

33. Porter and O'Donnell put it this way: "Context of Culture is instantiated in Context of Situation, in the same way that the Language System is instantiated in Text; Context of Culture is realized in Language as System, in the same way that Context of Situation is realized in Text" (*Discourse Analysis*, 126).

genre distinction could be between stories (i.e., narrative) and not stories (i.e., nonnarrative). At the same time, each culture has its common generic genres that share different degrees of similarity to the other cultures' genres. We expect similar structures, semantics, and lexicogrammar resources to be used whenever there are enough common situations that can be treated similarly for a culture and language. As Callow notes, "Within any given language community, there is widespread consensus (due to shared experiences and shared purposes) as to what needs to be mentioned and what does not. What is omitted is significant, as well as what is said."[34] Furthermore, different genres can be combined or embedded within a broad genre in any text.

One could use different terms to distinguish "universal" text types (e.g., narrative and nonnarrative), generic genres common to a culture, and more specific registers for particular situations.[35] To simplify the picture, I am using "genre" loosely to refer to generic cultural genres. In my mind, any text simultaneously conforms to some extent to generic genres and adapts them into unique combinations. A New Testament epistle, for example, may fall within the broad genre of an ancient Greco-Roman letter, with subgenres (primarily exhortation and exposition) combined and adapted to serve the specific situation.[36]

3. Variations in Situation

Ultimately, language use differs according to the situation.[37] For example, we might expect the same author to write a private letter to an individual differently than a public letter to a group. This is precisely what we find in Paul's letters. While his letters conform to the generic form of ancient Greco-Roman letters (with opening, body, and closing), they seem different depending on the situation. In a helpful survey of the generic structure potential of Paul's letters, Porter and O'Donnell suggest that Paul's letters have a five-part form: opening, thanksgiving, body, paraenesis, and closing, with thanksgiving and paraenesis optional. The church letters (other than Galatians) share all five parts. Apart from Galatians, it seems Paul was thankful in some form for the churches in various places. Personal letters differ in

---

34. Callow, *Man and Message* 3.2.4.3, "The Background of Familiarity."

35. See Porter and O'Donnell, *Discourse Analysis*, 148–54, 299–303.

36. Breeze characterizes the New Testament Epistles as "discourses consisting mainly of exhortation and exposition of doctrine. The overall message of each one is communicated by a combination of these genres and by the skillful weaving together of the various kinds of information constituting each type" ("Hortatory Discourse in Ephesians" 1, "Introduction").

37. Porter and O'Donnell, *Discourse Analysis*, 473, 490.

whether thanksgiving or paraenesis is excluded. It appears that Paul often did not need to express thanks or give extended theologically grounded moral appeals when dealing with personal friends or ministry companions. This difference in structure and meaning supports the common division into church and personal letters based on who is addressed. In the church letters, Paul and often a co-sender address a church or churches in the letter opening (with many second-person plural references throughout the letter). In the personal letters, Paul addresses individuals (there are no second-person plural references in Titus or 1 and 2 Timothy).[38]

In my opinion, thanksgiving and paraenesis are optional subsections within the letter body rather than optional sections on par with the letter opening, body, and closing. However, I agree with Porter and O'Donnell about the differences in situation, structure, and meaning. In my view, Paul usually starts the body of his letters by thanking God for specific aspects of the recipients' faith or behavior, which are directly related to significant themes he develops in the letter.[39] The content of the thanksgiving and the precise direction in which Paul develops his themes depend on each letter's situation. Likewise, Paul usually completes the body of his letters with extended exhortations appropriate for each circumstance. As we will see in the commentary, in the case of Galatians, both the absence of a thanksgiving subsection and repeated rounds of extended rebuke are significant and reflect the letter's situation.[40]

This situation variation is precisely why I insisted above that we must carefully analyze relevant texts individually and as a whole to understand the language, situation, and intended message. It is also the reason why I prioritize interpreting a text with other parts of itself.

---

38. Porter and O'Donnell, *Discourse Analysis*, 471–81. Only Philemon, which has Paul and Timothy addressing a group of individuals, does not fit neatly with this characterization of the personal letters.

39. See O'Brien, *Introductory Thanksgivings*.

40. Paul faced a situation where he knew that his views and exhortations would be contested. As Callow notes, a speaker "faces a very different situation if he knows that the hearer is either uninterested in the proposed activity or reluctant to carry it out. The situation becomes essentially a negotiable one, with the speaker trying to change the hearer's mind by a variety of devices—extolling the proposed activity, removing obstacles to its performance, persuading the hearer that bad results will not follow but good results will, and so on" (*Man and Message*, 7.3.2.1 "Directives").

4. Mainline or Support

In actual interpretation, the ability to discern the relative centrality of different discourse units is critical. Regardless of text type or situation, any text can be divided into mainline and supporting material. Porter and O'Donnell suggest viewing this in terms of horizontal and vertical dimensions. The horizontal mainline drives the text forward linearly, while the vertical material offers additional support and context. The mainline consists of all content along a linear path comprising main clauses. These clauses center on the predicates. The supporting material comprises all content outside the mainline, particularly subordinate clauses and various types of projected clauses (e.g., direct or indirect speech).[41] Callow sees this from the perspective of message core and message support. The message core advances the discourse's purpose, whether to convey information, prompt action, alter a situation, or express an attitude or emotion. The message support reinforces the core by aiding the listener's comprehension and acceptance.[42]

In hortatory discourse, the message core contains the information intended to prompt action. Commands and less direct exhortations carry it.[43] The message support may include anything that backs up these directives. It typically clarifies the commands, prevents misunderstandings, and encourages the audience to accept the directives more readily.[44]

My method is essentially an enhanced form of RST by tying discourse flow more closely with surface forms. It helps me distinguish between mainline and support and categorize the different types of support material. RST is ideal for our purposes because it complements other descriptive methods by design. Definitions are open and flexible, allowing easy adaptation to different situations and applications.[45]

In essence, RST posits that every part of a text has a role to play in relation to its other parts. These discourse relations explain why a text is coherent.[46] Since the 1980s, RST has been deployed with success in computational discourse parsing, which involves automatically analyzing and

---

41. Porter and O'Donnell, *Discourse Analysis*, 299.

42. Breeze, "Hortatory Discourse in Ephesians" 2.2, "Analysis of Nonnarrative Discourse." See further Callow, *Man and Message*, chs. 7–9.

43. Porter and O'Donnell suggest that "the imperative, subjunctive, and even optative may be used in contexts of commanding with increasing prominence" (*Discourse Analysis*, 330).

44. Breeze, "Hortatory Discourse in Ephesians" 2.2, "Analysis of Nonnarrative Discourse."

45. Taboada and Mann, "Rhetorical Structure Theory," 425.

46. Taboada and Mann, "Rhetorical Structure Theory," 425.

identifying the structure and relationships between different parts of a text.⁴⁷ This process usually involves:

1. Identifying discourse units (i.e., breaking the text into smaller segments like clauses or sentences)
2. Determining discourse relations (i.e., figuring out how different segments are connected, e.g., through causality, contrast, or elaboration)
3. Building discourse structure (i.e., constructing a representation of how all the segments fit together)⁴⁸

There are helpful parallels between this computational task and human discourse analysis.

With RST, we have a description framework that aids in dividing texts into units, combining units into larger spans, discovering the relationship between spans, discerning the writer's purposes, and evaluating which spans are more central to the writer's purposes.⁴⁹ It introduces the concepts of nuclei (central ideas) and satellites (supporting information), which share many similarities to the mainline and support or message core and message support distinctions. Nuclei are more essential to the writer's purpose than satellites. As Taboada and Mann note, "The satellite is often incomprehensible without the nucleus, whereas a text where the satellites have been deleted can be understood to a certain extent."⁵⁰ As conceived by Mann and Thompson, central ideas and supporting ideas are distinct from mainline and support in being defined by function and the text's writer's goals.⁵¹ When viewed within the framework of SFL that connects language, situation, and a writer's goals, I do not see a fundamental incompatibility between connecting form (i.e., the surface text) and function more consistently. Instead, RST is strengthened by systematically tracing these discourse relations to the text's surface forms, like explicitly signaled relations between clauses.⁵² We preserve the focus on concepts and functions as long as we recognize that multiple surface forms are used to achieve similar functions. At the same time, we benefit from having explicit criteria to appeal to in the lexicogrammar and semantics of a text when identifying discourse relations between different units of texts.

47. Taboada and Mann, "Rhetorical Structure Theory," 423; Zeldes et al., "eRST."
48. See Zeldes et al., "eRST."
49. Taboada and Mann, "Rhetorical Structure Theory," 445.
50. Taboada and Mann, "Rhetorical Structure Theory," 427.
51. Mann and Thompson, *Theory of Text Organization*, 39.
52. Zeldes et al. likewise point to the need to address this traditional weakness in RST when positing their version of enhanced RST ("eRST," 3, 5, 9).

B. Explaining the Method

The theoretical concepts above briefly explain why it is possible to move cautiously simultaneously across text, situation, language, and culture. They also recommend a text-based study focused on the text's lexicogrammar and semantics. This section will outline my method that flows out of this theoretical framework. The intent is to apply both a top-down and bottom-up systematic textual analysis.[53]

1. Determining Genre and Subgenres

The first step is to tentatively determine the broad genre of the text. If we are dealing with a letter, we can further compare and contrast with both typical Greco-Roman letter structure and Paul's letters.[54] If we are dealing with one of Paul's letters, grouping it with his letters to churches or individuals may be helpful.[55] The limited goal of this step is to gain some insight into the basic framework of the text.[56]

The next step is to identify the different subgenres within the book interpreted tentatively. For a letter, I would expect more nonnarrative than narrative. However, there may be narrative sections when the author recounts stories to support his exposition or exhortation.[57] Knowing where we are dealing with narrative or nonnarrative helps us distinguish mainline and supporting material. As Porter and O'Donnell note:

> Narrative usually contains the events, participants, and setting in the mainline material while supplemental material such as commentary or expansion or explanation is secondary. For the Hellenistic Greek speaker or writer, the aorist tense-form, especially (though not always) in the indicative mood form, characterizes the backbone of narrative texts, as central to the mainline or the storyline of the discourse. . . . Thus, in narrative sections of the

---

53. As Porter and O'Donnell note, top-down and bottom-up approaches "should work together in a check-and-balance relationship" (*Discourse Analysis*, 34).

54. Porter and O'Donnell helpfully note that opening, body, and closing are obligatory elements in Greco-Roman letters. They also argue that Paul's letters include two optional additional elements of thanksgiving and paraenesis (*Discourse Analysis*, 476–79).

55. See Porter and O'Donnell, *Discourse Analysis*, 471–81.

56. For how I practically did this, see my comments in "Letter Opening: Setting the Scene" (1:1–5); "Rebuke and Changing Perceptions" (1:6–9); and "Letter Closing" (6:11–18).

57. As we shall see, this definitely happens in Galatians.

Gospels, and other Greek narrative literature, the backbone of the narrative is carried by a string of aorist indicative verbs in primary clauses.... In nonnarrative sections of the Gospels, as well as most sections of the letters of the New Testament, and speeches from a variety of ancient Greek literature, the mainline of the discourse is often carried by a string of imperfective aspect and present tense–form verbs in primary clauses, unless narrative is being created. Secondary clauses, projections, and related structures (such as infinitives and participles in nonprimary clausal components) are used to develop further ideas within the text, such as the purpose or result of actions.[58]

In my experience interpreting Paul's letters, careful observation of how exposition and exhortation intersect pays excellent dividends. For any given part of the text, ask: Is Paul more concerned with informing his audience (exposition) or getting them to do something (exhortation)?

From a top-down perspective, the broad genre of Galatians appears to be hortatory. Even though there is a fair amount of exposition, they seem to support the rebukes and exhortations that run throughout the mainline of the letter. Moreover, the heavy concentration of rebuke in Galatians hints at the likelihood that distinguishing rebukes from exhortations might yield valuable insights. For this reason, I employed Callow's three "imports" of language to distinguish rebukes from exhortations. Under this scheme, exposition falls under informationals (i.e., giving or requesting information), exhortation under volitionals (i.e., instigating action or changing states of affairs), or rebuke under expressives (i.e., expressing emotions and opinions).[59]

2. Finding Clues to High-Level Boundaries

This second step aims to discern tentative clues to high-level boundaries from a big-picture perspective.[60] At a high level, looking for significant

---

58. Porter and O'Donnell, *Discourse Analysis*, 302–3.

59. Callow, *Man and Message* 7.3, "The Three Imports." Informationals and volitionals correspond to the two interpersonal metafunctions of transmission of information and negotiating action in SFL studies of discourse exchange structure (see Porter and O'Donnell, *Discourse Analysis*, 139).

60. This step corresponds to Levinsohn's steps of determining the major divisions of the discourse and finding surface features that support different boundaries ("Discourse Analysis: Galatians," 112–14). The only difference is that I would not start with looking at agreements and disagreements among exegetes about boundaries. However, I do agree that these provide a useful comparison. In addition, it is often helpful to pay attention to the kind of surface features Levinsohn lists as potential boundary indicators.

changes in discourse markers, clusters of meanings, participants, and even text types is helpful. Discourse markers often signal where paragraphs begin and end and how they connect to the surrounding text. In addition, paragraphs are bound together by cohesion and segmented from one another. This means that topic shifts between paragraphs are typically discernible. This frequently includes changes in the interaction between the author and the audience from one paragraph to the next. Furthermore, paragraphs may embody various literary text types, such as narrative or exposition.[61]

I assume that we can discern different levels of discourse units above the clause or sentence level based on some form of thematic unity. This is grounded in the need speakers and writers have to "order and group their message . . . to make it more understandable to their hearers and readers."[62] For convenience's sake, I often use the word "paragraph" to refer to groups of higher discourse units. Crucially, I do not see paragraphs as one fixed set, all on the same level. Instead, I think multiple paragraphs can recursively combine to form larger groupings of paragraphs.[63] Some paragraphs may also be subdivided into smaller paragraphs.[64] Because of this recursive nature, I will sometimes refer to both paragraphs and groupings of paragraphs as simply paragraphs (with the understanding that there are different levels of paragraphs). Sometimes, I will refer to paragraph groupings as paragraph groups (or more informally as a section) when it is relevant to highlight the more extensive grouping.

The six paragraph groups I use to organize the next six chapters in this commentary represent the highest discourse units I found helpful below the epistolary structure of letter opening, body, and closing. The different levels of headings and subheadings usually correspond to varying levels of meaningful paragraph groupings.[65] I spelled out what I saw as the main point for each paragraph group or paragraph in these headings and subheadings.

---

61. See Porter and O'Donnell, *Discourse Analysis*, 244–45, which suggests seven general characteristics that help define paragraphs.

62. Porter and O'Donnell, *Discourse Analysis*, 216.

63. Beekman and Callow talk about semantic paragraphs and sections (*Translating Word of God*, 275–76). Longacre speaks of paragraphs as recursive in nature, including nestings of paragraph within paragraph ("Exhortation and Mitigation," 4). See Callow, *Man and Message* 10.2.1, "The Message as a Patterned Hierarchy."

64. Neeley notes that: "Especially in long discourses, paragraphs combine to form sections (cf. chapters in a novel). . . . At times, these embedded discourses themselves are quite long and may be divided into their own sections composed of paragraphs (cf. sections in the chapter of a novel)" ("Discourse Analysis of Hebrews," s.vv. "Units in the Discourse").

65. This chapter and the chapter on the letter opening are the most notable exceptions.

To make an analogy, in this step, I aim to build my own outline or table of contents to gain a bird's-eye view of the discourse. It must be noted that these initial impressions are preparatory, suggestive, and subject to iterative revision as we engage in a ground-up analysis of how clauses, paragraphs, and paragraph groups are related.[66]

3. Tracing the Flow

If the assumption that some theme unifies higher-level discourse units like paragraphs is granted, then our first task is to trace how themes are developed. One good place to start is to focus on the finite verbs and assign clauses with finite verbs as either part of the mainline or support. We would evaluate each of these verbs to determine its role in the discourse—whether it advances the theme or serves a supporting function.[67] Supporting material frequently follows the mainline it supports. However, it also can precede the mainline. For example, when an inference is drawn, the support comes first and serves as the basis for the inference.[68] In addition, there can be multiple levels of support. For each paragraph posited, test to see if you can come up with a heading that plausibly sums up the paragraph's main point with the supporting material removed.[69] This would often be one of the main clauses, though it could be multiple coordinated clauses that are equally central.[70] At the same time, make sure you can plausibly account for how all other materials omitted support it. These often go on recursively as each paragraph has its own main point, but a paragraph could also serve as support for another paragraph group. Each paragraph group would also have its own main point (which often corresponds to the main point of the central paragraph in the group).

---

66. Runge is particularly helpful on how different Greek connectives and other discourse features function (*Discourse Grammar*). Runge's insights often inform my application of a form of enhanced RST to trace the discourse flow.

67. Beekman and Callow, *Translating Word of God*, 323.

68. See Schreiner, *Interpreting the Pauline Epistles*, 104.

69. This is in line with RST's view that the writer's central ideas can be understood to some extent even when all the supporting ideas are removed (but not vice versa). See Taboada and Mann, "Rhetorical Structure Theory," 426–27; Mann and Thompson, *Theory of Text Organization*, 32–34.

70. Sometimes, the main point could also be implicit. For example, when a question is asked and the answer is obvious, the implied answer may be the main point developed further, not the question itself. As Beekman and Callow note, "Implicit information is frequently found in conversational sequences. These sequences may be in the form of direct or indirect speech, or they may be statements or question-answer sequences. Generally the question or statement introduces information which is left implicit in the response" (*Translating Word of God*, 50).

For the New Testament Epistles, connectives and lexical choices are the evidence I will point to most frequently. As Paul's letters are rich in conjunctions, I usually start by carefully tracing how these connectives connect up each clause. However, not all relations are signaled by an explicit connective. We must account for other means used to connect clauses and paragraphs. For convenience's sake, I refer to this more extensive set of lexicogrammatical features that provide cohesive connections simply as connectors. I use a broad term of closely related concepts to refer to connections through lexical choices. These include synonyms, antonyms, repetitions, and words within the same semantic domain.[71] Beyond words, combined lexical choices can also signal broader associations like expected answers to questions or natural responses in light of the situation. Table 1 below summarizes how I interpret the connectors in Galatians.[72]

Table 1: Connectors in Galatians		
Connector	Function	Typical Use
ἀλλά	Corrects	Corrects expectation or information in contrast to previous
ἄρα	Infers	Infers a point from the previous assumption or argument
γάρ	Supports	Supports or strengthens what precedes
δέ	Elaborates	Adds a distinct point that advances the argument
Demonstrative	Refers	When backward pointing, can link to multiple previous clauses
διό	Infers	Infers a point from the previous assumption or argument

71. See Beekman and Callow, *Translating Word of God*, 323. Besides cohesion through connectives and lexical choices, two more types of cohesive ties identified by Halliday and Hasan are noteworthy: reference (e.g., pronouns, demonstratives, comparisons) and ellipsis (e.g., omission of an item that can be recovered from the context) (*Cohesion in English*, 4). Their other category of substitution can be merged within reference or lexical choice.

72. This is similar to how Levinsohn considers the implications of each inter-sentential conjunction. Levinsohn provides a helpful list of the constraints associated with many of the conjunctions found in Galatians ("Discourse Analysis: Galatians," 115–16). See also Runge, *Discourse Grammar*, ch. 2, "Connecting Conjunctions." There are two main differences here. First, I have tried to simplify further Levinsohn's and Runge's terminology. Second, my table expands the list of connectors considered. Another helpful resource on asyndeton and sentence conjunctions is Black, *Sentence Conjunctions*. I view Levinsohn, Runge, and Black as all holding to a minimalist view of the role of sentence conjunctions in discourse, with which I agree.

εἰ μή	Exception	Adds back in an exception after all members of set removed
ἔπειτα	Next	Next in chronological sequence
ἵνα	Purpose	Purpose of previous assertion
καί	Associates	Adds an associated point in parallel to previous point
καθώς	Compares	Compares to an analogous situation
μόνον	Exception	Adds an exception
None	Break	No conjunction (asyndeton) and no closely related concepts signal major or minor breaks
ὅτι	Reason	Reason supporting previous
οὖν	Infers	Infers a distinct point that advances the argument
οὕτως καί	Compares	Infers that a situation is analogous in comparison
Closely related concept	Associates	No conjunction (asyndeton), but adds a closely associated point. Lexical or conceptual repetition may be used to indicate closely related concepts in immediately adjacent clauses. However, it includes broader associations like answers to questions or natural responses to the situation.
Relative clause	Defines	Further defines or redefines
ὥστε	Result	Result inferred from previous point

Regarding conjunctions, I highlight their function only when they join clauses or paragraphs.[73] When καί, δέ, and ἀλλά are connecting independent clauses, they function to indicate different degrees of continuity or discontinuity.[74] Most conjunctions that serve a logical-semantic function (e.g., comparative, local, temporal, conditional, inferential, causal, purpose, or result) connect subordinate clauses to independent clauses.[75] However, some conjunctions also serve a logical-semantic function between groups

---

73. For example, καί can also join together words or groups of words. On the different levels that discourse conjunctions can serve, see Porter and O'Donnell, "Conjunctions, Clines, and Levels," 8–10.

74. On the cline of continuity-discontinuity, see Porter and O'Donnell, "Conjunctions, Clines, and Levels," 10–11.

75. Coordination or parataxis signals that clauses thus connected belong together, either on the mainline or as support. The clauses may be of equal importance, or conjoined clauses may provide some form of elaboration. Subordination or hypotaxis signals that the clauses subordinated are supporting material. See Taboada and Mann, "Rhetorical Structure Theory," 427.

of independent clauses or paragraphs. These are the conjunctions I have labeled as "Supports" or "Infers" in function.[76]

When no conjunctions link clauses (asyndeton), I also indicate where other connectors exist. Specifically, I see demonstratives or closely related concepts indicating textual continuity. In the "Function" column, I briefly specify the nature of the closely related concept. For example, I include lexical or conceptual repetition in adjacent clauses under closely related concepts. In such cases, despite the lack of a conjunction, we have a close connection rather than a break. I enter "None" in the "Connectors" column in my tables only when there are no connectors of any kind. Those places correspond to a major or minor break. Notably, a break in a text's linear development does not mean there are no cohesive links to other parts of the text. I will also point out in my comments when lexical or conceptual repetition links different parts of the text (even across large distances) in a nonsequential way.[77]

Furthermore, we should examine how clusters of meaning flow from one paragraph to another (including what unanswered questions or underdeveloped themes in a paragraph are developed further in the next). Repeating top-down (see "Determining Genre and Subgenres" and "Finding Clues to High-Level Boundaries" above) and bottom-up (see "Tracing the Flow" here) approaches is often necessary to refine the results. This process can be repeated as often as needed until you reach the point of diminishing returns for your specific purpose.

My aim in going through the above-mentioned process is to examine the text from multiple angles and perspectives. The process cannot be fully shown in this commentary step by step. This is because there was a lot of going back and forth between top-down and bottom-up steps as I continually refined my analysis through multiple rounds. So, I sought to provide the next best thing within the constraints of print. First, I reproduced the main questions I asked as I examined the text. As you read this commentary, you

---

76. I generally agree with the tentative suggestion Porter and O'Donnell made that conjunctions (1) mark the degree of continuity-discontinuity in a text's linear development between primary (i.e., independent) clauses; and (2) indicate how secondary (subordinate) clauses support, develop, or explain the primary clauses ("Conjunctions, Clines, and Levels," 13). However, I would include γάρ and οὖν as serving a logical-semantic function rather than continuity-discontinuity.

77. Distinguishing noncontiguous lexical and conceptual connections will help us avoid accidentally confusing textual cohesion across the whole text with continuity in the linear development of the text. This is because groups of clauses or paragraphs that start with a major or minor break from the immediately preceding group of clauses or paragraphs may still use lexical or conceptual repetition to tie to other more distant parts of the text.

will ask the same questions I did. Second, I supplied tables that help trace the flow of the higher levels of the text. Third, I focus my main discussion on describing every step of the textual flow. This includes details about the relationship between groups of clauses and subordinate clauses that I purposely do not represent in the tables (as the tables become less helpful when they get too large and complex). These will be the primary means by which I guide you through the questions I asked and explain the connections I made.

C. Overall Letter Flow

One pivotal insight I gained from reading and rereading Galatians using the method outlined above was how rebuke and exhortations dominated the mainline of the discourse.[78] Once I recognized how Paul breaks into rebuke and keeps returning for a second, third, and even fourth round, it transformed my interpretation of the overall structure. Essentially, I discovered that the letter is broadly hortatory in genre, where rebukes and exhortations constitute the theme line of the letter.[79] Between the opening and closing, I found that the body consists of four rounds of rebuke, with the fourth round embedded within extended exhortation. At the highest level, my analysis yielded the following outline:

1. Letter Opening: Setting the Scene (1:1–5)
2. First Round of Rebuke, Backed by Extended Support (1:6—2:21)
3. Second Round of Rebuke, Backed by Extended Support (3:1—4:7)
4. Third Round of Rebuke (4:8–31)
5. Extended Exhortation with Fourth Round of Rebuke Embedded (5:1—6:10)
6. Letter Closing (6:11–18)

Instead of grouping my analysis according to the traditional six chapters, I will organize my discussion of the letter according to these six sections. Within these large sections, I will also use different levels of headings to show how I understand the subsections fitting together. At the highest level of the discourse, the five points between the letter opening and closing are:

---

78. As Porter and O'Donnell note, mainline and supporting material represent the two basic ways material is presented in a text (*Discourse Analysis*, 299).

79. Similarly, Levinsohn, "Discourse Analysis: Galatians," 112.

1. I am astonished that you are so quickly turning away from the divine gospel brought to you by a divinely appointed servant of Christ.
2. O foolish Galatians, I want to learn from you whether you received the Spirit through doing what the law requires or through hearing accompanied by faith.
3. How can you return again to the weak and poor elements?
4. Stand firm in freedom, and do not be subject again to slavery!
5. Walk by the Spirit, and you will not carry out the desire of the flesh.

Galatians' overall main point, which the rebukes support, is the appeal to stand firm in freedom and not be subject again to slavery. A coordinated second main point is the exhortation to walk by the Spirit, with the assurance that by doing so, the Galatians will not carry out the desire of the flesh. Despite starting their Christian experience in the Spirit, the Galatians were tempted to complete the Christian journey in the flesh through circumcision and doing what the law requires. So, Paul's primary purpose is to rebuke them and get them back on track. The appeal to stand firm in freedom (the positive side of the coin) and not be subject again to slavery (the negative side) can adequately account for almost all the letter's content, except for the extended exhortation in 5:1—6:10. It can serve as a more satisfactory summary of the overall main point for Galatians than any other major points Paul makes. In addition, Paul adds a second main point to address the Galatians' concern about completing their Christian journey (hinted at in 3:3 and developed in 5:1—6:10). The call to walk by the Spirit and the accompanying assurance that by doing so, the Galatians will not carry out the desire of the flesh offers a suitable summary of Paul's offered alternative (over against circumcision and doing what the law requires). It can serve as a more appropriate summary of Paul's second main point than other significant points made in 5:1—6:10.

Since the bottom-up details are complex, it is better to let you work through them with me as we read the text together. You can evaluate for yourself whether things match up when analyzed from the bottom up.

D. Outline

As previously mentioned, the body consists of four rounds of rebuke (II, III, IV, and V). I did not use a separate level for the body to reduce the number of layers.

    I. Letter Opening (1:1–5)

A. Setting the Scene (1:1–2)

B. Grace and Peace Come from Jesus Rescuing Us from the Present Evil Age (1:3–5)

II. First Round of Rebuke, Backed by Extended Support (1:6—2:21)

A. Rebuke and Changing Perceptions (1:6–9)

1. Undermining the "Other Gospel" (1:6–7)

2. Curse Pronouncement (1:8–9)

B. Paul Is a Servant of Christ and Proclaims a Divine Rather Than Human Gospel (1:10—2:21)

1. Transition to Support: Serving Christ as Justification for Opposing False Gospel (1:10)

2. Supporting Premises: Paul Proclaims a Divine Rather Than Human Gospel (1:11–12)

3. Supporting Evidence from Paul's Life and Ministry (1:13—2:21)

a. Did Not Consult with Others or Seek Affirmation After Conversion (1:13–17)

b. Had Only Limited Interaction with Two Apostles on Eventual Visit (1:18–20)

c. Remained Absent from Jerusalem While Judean Churches Affirmed His Gospel from Afar (1:21–24)

d. James, Cephas, and John Affirmed Paul's Gospel and Added Nothing to It (2:1–10)

e. Confronted and Corrected Cephas When He Obscured Truth of the Gospel (2:11–21)

III. Second Round of Rebuke, Backed by Extended Support (3:1—4:7)

A. Double-Layered Rebuke (3:1–6)

B. Only Those Who Rely on Faith Are Abraham's True Heirs (3:7—4:7)

1. Only Those Who Rely on Faith Are Blessed Together with Believing Abraham (3:7–14)

2. The Inheritance Does Not Rely on Law, but Rather on a Promise (3:15—4:7)

a. The Law Does Not Invalidate a Covenant Already Validated by God (3:15–18)

       b. The Law Confines All Under Sin in Service of the Promise (3:19–22)

       c. The Law Serves as a Guardian, Directing to Christ as the Destination (3:23–29)

       d. Believers Are No Longer Slaves Under the Law, but Rather Sons and Thus Heirs (4:1–7)

IV. Third Round of Rebuke (4:8–31)

    A. It Is Inconceivable for the Galatians to Return to Weak and Poor Elements (4:8–11)

    B. Become Like Paul, Just as Paul Had Become Like the Galatian Christians (4:12–20)

    C. Call to Listen to the Law and Recognize That They Are Children of the Free Woman, Children of Promise Like Isaac (4:21–31)

V. Extended Exhortation with Fourth Round of Rebuke Embedded (5:1—6:10)

    A. Stand Firm in Freedom, and Do Not Be Subject Again to Slavery (5:1–15)

    B. Walk in the Spirit, and You Will Not Carry Out the Desire of the Flesh (5:16–26)

    C. Let Us Work What Is Good for All, While We Have the Opportunity (6:1–10)

VI. Letter Closing (6:11–18)

    A. Parting Contrast Between Paul and the Opponents (6:11–17)

    B. Closing Benediction (6:18)

GALATIANS 1:1–5

OUTLINE

I. Letter Opening (1:1–5)

   A. Setting the Scene (1:1–2)

   B. Grace and Peace Come from Jesus Rescuing Us from the Present Evil Age (1:3–5)

I. LETTER OPENING (1:1–5)

Table 2 below shows the main elements of the letter opening:

Table 2: Main Elements of the Letter Opening		
What	Where	Function
Paul and all the brothers and sisters with him	1:1–2	Sender (unusual extended role description for Paul)
The churches in Galatia	1:2	Recipients
Prayer wish	1:3–4	Greeting (unusual extended role description for Jesus)
Doxology	1:5	Praise (unusual for a letter opening)

First of all, how does Paul's letter compare to typical letters in his day? Second, what can we learn from this comparison? The answer: the letter's opening largely adheres to ancient Greco-Roman conventions. However, two of Paul's deviations from these norms emphasize two key points in Galatians 1:1–5. First, Paul provides an unusually detailed description of his own role, highlighting his authority as an apostle, appointed not by human beings, but by Jesus Christ and God the Father. Second, Paul gives an expanded depiction of Jesus's role, focusing on his obedient sacrifice to rescue us from this present evil age. The third deviation to praise God highlights God the Father's role alongside Jesus in devising and desiring this rescue.

These points lay the groundwork (i.e., provide background support) for the entire letter. Why should the Galatians listen to Paul? He speaks with the authority of Jesus and God. Why should they return to the good news Paul preaches and reject the false gospel? Paul reminds them that God's purpose in Jesus's sacrificial giving of himself at the cross is to rescue his people from the present evil age. As he will make clear in the letter body, the so-called good news is part of this evil age, from which they have already been delivered. This is a compelling reason not to revert to those weak and impoverished elements.

A. Setting the Scene (1:1–2)

Today, letters generally begin simply with a greeting to their recipients. You usually must look at the envelope's return address or check the letter's end to find out who sent it. In ancient times, however, senders of letters typically began by identifying themselves and their addressees while greeting them. Paul both follows and diverges from the standard letter-writing conventions of his day. It is helpful to understand how he conforms to and breaks conventions. In the opening of the Letter to the Galatians, Paul identifies himself as writing to the churches of Galatia and greets them with a wish for grace and peace. This basic structure conforms to ancient Greco-Roman letter conventions. It is standard for letters to open with the sender, recipients, and a greeting.

The presence of a doxology in the opening of a letter is unusual, even for Paul.[1] After giving an expanded description of God's planned rescue of both himself and his recipients through Christ, Paul seems to have naturally responded with praise.[2] If Paul responds with praise, by implication, his recipients should too, since they share in God's blessing.[3] Another effect of adding this doxology here is to extend the description of God the Father's role (as deserving glory). In the context where what Jesus did is described

---

1. Van Voorst, "No Thanksgiving Period," 170–71.
2. Moo, *Galatians*, s.vv. "Prescript" (Gal 1:1–5).
3. Van Voorst suggests that with ἀμήν Paul engages the Galatians to respond with their own ἀμήν, implying: "Can you bless God with me for providing the death of Jesus Christ as the act that rescues us from the present evil age?" ("No Thanksgiving Period," 171).

as "according to the will of our God and Father," the practical effect is to underline God the Father's role in devising and desiring this rescue.

In addition, while the sender, recipient, and greeting elements are standard, Paul does expand on them in unusual ways. Next, we will examine each of these elements in more depth.

1. Role of Author: Paul

The author identifies himself as Paul, the apostle. This claim is not seriously challenged.[4] Who is Paul? Like Cephas, Paul was born a Jew (2:15). Paul was very zealous in the practice of his ancestral traditions, advancing in Judaism beyond many of his Jewish contemporaries (1:14). He also persecuted the church intensely and tried to destroy it (1:13). This is consistent with the portrayal in the Acts of the Apostles. There we learn that Paul is the Roman name of Saul (Acts 13:9), who was a Jew from a family of Pharisees (Acts 23:6). He was born in Tarsus of Cilicia (Acts 9:11; 21:39; 22:3). However, he was brought up in Jerusalem and studied under Gamaliel (Acts 22:3), a highly respected teacher of the law among the Pharisees (Acts 5:34–40). Saul the Pharisee was a persecutor of the church. He asked for letters from the high priest in Jerusalem to the synagogues in Damascus to authorize him to arrest the believers there and bring them to Jerusalem to be punished (Acts 9:1–2; 22:4–5). However, God, who divinely appointed him before he was born, was pleased to reveal his Son to him (Gal 1:15–16). This would correspond well to Paul's conversion experience on the Damascus road recounted in Acts (9:1–19; 22:1–21; 26:1–23). The purpose of God's call is that Paul might proclaim Christ among the gentiles (Gal 1:16).

After learning a little about Paul's background, the next question is how Paul portrays himself in the letter. Beyond naming the sender and receiver to remove any ambiguity about who they are, Paul tends to add extra descriptive information about them in his letter openings. Galatians is no exception. This is one way Paul often adapts his greetings to suit each letter's unique circumstances and conditions.[5] For example, in most of his letters, Paul identifies himself as an apostle of Christ Jesus. He explains how he gained this position, such as "through the will of God" (1 Cor 1:1; 2 Cor 1:1; Eph 1:1; Col 1:1; 2 Tim 1:1).[6] In the Letter to the Philippians, Paul describes himself and Timothy as slaves rather than apostles in the greeting. On the one hand, this social designation sets the social and interpersonal context

---

4. See, e.g., DeSilva, *Galatians*, 1.
5. George, *Galatians*, 76.
6. Schreiner, *Galatians*, 73.

for that letter, depicting Paul and Timothy as having serving roles.[7] On the other hand, it connects Paul and Timothy thematically to the letter's overall message about putting others' needs before one's own.[8]

Nevertheless, the initial greetings in Paul's Letter to the Romans and his Letter to the Galatians are remarkable because they are significantly longer than usual. As in Romans, the distinctive elements in the opening of Galatians foreshadow significant themes in the letter.[9] Notably, Paul spends almost as much time describing what kind of apostle he is not as what kind he is (1:1).[10]

By ruling out the potential human basis for his apostleship ("neither from humans nor by humans"), he effectively underscores Christ's and God's positive agency ("through Jesus Christ and God the Father who raised him from the dead").[11] Notably, Paul took pains to clarify the origins of his apostolic appointment first before identifying the addressees. At the outset, Paul already lays the groundwork for correcting apparent misperceptions. In so doing, he sets the stage for his rigorous assertion that his apostleship derives from God and Christ rather than from human beings in 1:11—2:21.[12]

If we look ahead, we will learn much about Paul's journeys, interactions, beliefs, and practices from Paul's abundant personal (i.e., first-person) references. In table 3 below, all references to Paul are listed at a glance. The references are distinguished into noun references, pronoun references, and cases where Paul is the implied subject of verbs.[13]

---

7. On how explicit social designations and speech roles within the discourse both express the social exchange that Paul sees happening (or desires to happen) between him and his readers, see Reed, *Discourse Analysis of Philippians*, 181–92.

8. Runge, *Galatians*, Gal 1:1–5.

9. Schreiner, *Galatians*, 71; DeSilva, *Galatians*, 112; Moo, *Galatians*, s.vv. "Prescript" (Gal 1:1–5).

10. Moo notes that only in Galatians does Paul set his "divine calling [as an apostle] in contrast to any possible human derivation" (*Galatians*, s.vv. "Prescript" [Gal 1:1–5]).

11. Moo has a helpful discussion of the use of ἀπό and διά with humans and only διά with Jesus Christ and God the Father (*Galatians*, s.vv. "Prescript" [Gal 1:1–5]). I am also inclined to see Paul ruling out any human source or agency and highlighting the agency of Christ and God.

12. Van Voorst notes that the unusualness of what Paul has done here and that he has already begun to signal that he is not writing a happy letter here in 1:1 ("No Thanksgiving Period," 167).

13. Both noun and pronoun references are explicit references. Pronoun references have reduced semantic value in comparison to noun references. Implicit references implied by the verb are at the bottom of the hierarchy. See further Porter and O'Donnell, *Discourse Analysis*, 430–31.

Table 3: Paul as a Participant in the Overall Letter		
Noun References	Pronoun References	Implied Subject of Verbs
1:1 (Παῦλος), 23 (ὁ διώκων ἡμᾶς ποτε)	1:2, 3, 4 (3x), 8, 11, 12, 13, 14 (2x), 15 (2x), 16, 17, 24	1:6, 8, 9 (2x), 10 (5x), 11, 12, 13 (2x), 14 (2x), 16 (2x), 17 (3x), 18 (3x), 19, 20 (2x), 21, 22, 23
	2:2, 3, 4 (2x), 6 (2x), 8, 9 (3x), 15, 16, 17, 18, 19, 20 (4x)	2:1 (2x), 2 (5x), 4, 5, 7, 10 (3x), 11, 14 (2x), 16 (2x), 17 (2x), 18 (3x), 19 (2x), 20 (2x), 21
	3:13 (2x), 24	3:2 (2x), 14, 15, 17, 23 (2x), 24, 25
	4:3, 6, 12 (3x), 14 (2x), 15, 18, 19, 20, 21, 26	4:1, 3, 5, 11 (2x), 12, 13, 15, 16 (2x), 19, 20 (4x), 31
5:2 (Παῦλος)	5:1, 2, 5, 10, 11, 26 (2x)	5:3, 11, 16, 21 (2x), 25 (2x), 26 (3x)
	6:11, 14 (4x), 17 (3x), 18	6:9 (4x), 10 (2x), 11

What insights can we gain at this high level? First, Paul appears to be a significant participant throughout the letter. Second, Paul is the most personally involved in chs. 1, 2, and 4. To deepen our analysis, let us separate out first-person plural references. In table 4 below, I will use my paragraph headings to give a sense of the nature of the paragraphs where these first-person plural references occur.

Table 4: First-Person Plural References to Paul and the Churches of Galatia		
Pronoun References	Implied Subject of Verbs	Paragraph Heading
1:3, 4 (3x)		1:1–5 Letter Opening
2:4 (2x)	2:4	2:1–10 James, Cephas, and John Affirmed Paul's Gospel and Added Nothing to It
3:13 (2x)	3:14	3:7–14 Only Those Who Rely on Faith Are Blessed Together with Believing Abraham
3:24	3:23 (2x), 24, 25	3:23–29: The Law Serves as a Guardian, Directing to Christ as the Destination
4:3, 6	4:3, 5	4:1–7: Believers Are No Longer Slaves Under the Law, but Rather Sons and Thus Heirs
4:26	4:31	4:21–31: Call to Listen to the Law and Recognize That They Are Children of the Free Woman, Children of Promise Like Isaac

5:1, 5		5:1–15: Stand Firm in Freedom, and Do Not Be Subject Again to Slavery
5:26 (2x)	5:25 (2x), 26 (3x)	5:16–26: Walk in the Spirit, and You Will Not Carry Out the Desire of the Flesh
	6:9 (4x), 10 (2x)	6:1–10: Let Us Work What Is Good for All, While We Have the Opportunity
6:14, 18		6:11–18: Letter Closing

It appears that Paul usually employs first-person plural pronouns to include his audience as agreeing or participating together with him in some aspect of the gospel message. First-person plurals appear in the exposition paragraphs. Notably, except for 5:1–15, they are absent from the rebuke paragraphs (see table 9, "Second-Person Plural References").

After considering the first-person plural references, let us turn our attention to first-person singular references to Paul. In table 5 below, only such first-person singular references are considered.

Table 5: First-Person Singular References to Paul	
Pronoun References	Implied Subject of Verbs
1:2, 11, 12, 13, 14 (2x), 15 (2x), 16, 17, 24	1:6, 9, 10 (5x), 11, 12, 13 (2x), 14 (2x), 16 (2x), 17 (3x), 18 (3x), 19, 20 (2x), 21, 22, 23
2:2, 3, 6 (2x), 8, 9 (2x), 18, 19, 20 (4x)	2:1 (2x), 2 (5x), 7, 10 (2x), 11, 14 (2x), 18 (3x), 19 (2x), 20 (2x), 21
	3:2 (2x), 15, 17
4:12 (3x), 14 (2x), 15, 18, 19, 20, 21	4:1, 11 (2x), 12, 13, 15, 16 (2x), 19, 20 (4x)
5:2, 10, 11	5:3, 11, 16, 21 (2x)
6:11, 14, 17 (3x)	6:11

The heaviest concentration of first-person singular references corresponds to the section where Paul portrays himself as a servant of Christ and as proclaiming a divine rather than human gospel. In this section, Paul recounts his call and early interactions (or lack thereof) with the Jerusalem apostles in support (1:10—2:21). This included confronting an erring Cephas in Antioch (2:11–21). In addition, his earlier ministry with the Galatians supports his call for them to emulate him (4:12–20).

Most of the remaining first-person singular references occur in the places where Paul cites his own beliefs and practices to support his message

(2:18–21; 5:11; 6:14, 17).[14] This includes his willingness to be persecuted by no longer advocating circumcision (5:11), for which he has experienced much trouble and personal suffering (6:17). Instead, he upholds the good news of a crucified Messiah where what matters is a new creation rather than circumcision (6:14–15).

Besides Paul, were others involved in sending the letter? Before mentioning the recipients, Paul includes "all the brothers and sisters who are with me" (1:2) as senders. While Paul often names co-authors (Sosthenes in 1 Cor 1:1; Timothy in 2 Cor 1:1; Phil 1:1; Col 1:1; Phlm 1; Silas and Timothy in 1 Thess 1:1; 2 Thess 1:1), only in Galatians does he include an undefined group. By being named co-senders, they are depicted as agreeing with Paul's views. It may refer only to multiple ministry associates. However, given that Paul usually refers to fellow Christians with ἀδελφοί, it likely refers more generally to all the believers who are with him as he writes the letter.[15] This signals that the larger Christian community stands in solidarity with Paul and supports his appeal to the Galatians.[16]

2. Role of Recipients: The Churches of Galatia

After spelling out the divine origins of his apostolic appointment and co-opting his fellow believers as co-senders, Paul finally identifies the intended audience as the churches of Galatia (1:2). This is the only letter in which Paul explicitly names multiple churches as recipients.[17]

Who were the Galatians? What do we know about them? In Paul's day, the Roman province of Galatia included many ethnic groups and sizable territories.[18] The northern part historically belonged to the Celtic people (or ethnic Galatians), which Paul might or might not have ministered to during his so-called second and third missionary journeys (Acts 16:6; 18:23).[19] The

---

14. See, e.g., Moo, *Galatians*, s.vv. "Introduction to Galatians." Note also that this pattern of Paul using first-person singular references in juxtaposition to opponents (2:14–21; 5:7–12; 6:12–17) would seem to support Hardin's thesis that Paul offers himself as a foil to contrast himself with his opponents ("Galatians 1–2 Without a Mirror"). Note that in 2:14–21, I am viewing Cephas as temporarily falling into the category of an opponent.

15. In the absence of explicit reasons to exclude them, all first-person plural references will always include these co-senders. Because they are included by default, there was no need to include a separate table for them.

16. Moo, *Galatians*, s.vv. "Prescript" (Gal 1:1–5).

17. Runge, *Galatians*, Gal 1:1–5.

18. DeSilva, *Galatians*, 3.

19. Moo, *Galatians*, s.vv. "Introduction to Galatians."

southern part included notable cities like Pisidian Antioch, Iconium, Lystra, and Derbe, to which Paul ministered during his first missionary journey with Barnabas, according to Acts 13–14.[20]

There is some interpretive significance to whether Gal 2:1–10 is seen as referring to the same events as Acts 15. If you accept the historicity of Acts (which I do), then Paul would apparently have omitted any mention of the famine relief visit to Jerusalem (Acts 11:27–30; 12:25). With the focus on absence or presence in Jerusalem and absence of interaction with the apostles in Jerusalem in Gal 1:13—2:21, I find it unlikely that Paul would omit this visit as it would undermine his claims of independence from the Jerusalem church and the Jerusalem apostles.[21] In addition, Paul is happy to emphasize that the pillars of the Jerusalem church recognized and affirmed the divine origin of his message and calling (2:7–9). Even though he first clarified that they added nothing to him and that their importance in human eyes does not matter to God either (2:6), Paul still marshals their affirmation to support this case. It seems likely that, if it were an option, Paul would have strengthened his case further by explicitly appealing to the decision from the Jerusalem Council in Acts 15.[22] So, I am inclined to conclude that the Jerusalem Council had not happened yet when Paul wrote Galatians.[23] Instead, I would match the visit in Gal 1:18–19 with Acts 9:26–29 and Gal 2:1–10 with Acts 11:27–30. While there are many similarities between the meeting in Gal 2:1–10 and Acts 15:1–29, I see two distinct events with similar themes. The former was a private meeting that yielded an informal understanding. The latter was a public discussion and delivered a formal decision.[24] Given that we know that Paul ministered in southern Galatia prior to the Jerusalem Council, I lean towards identifying the churches of Galatia as located in southern Galatia, including especially the churches Paul planted in Acts 13–14 in Pisidian Antioch, Iconium, Lystra, and Derbe.

What about what Paul says about his audience and how he portrays them? In table 6 below, all references to the churches of Galatia are listed at a glance. The references are distinguished into noun references, pronoun references, and cases where the churches of Galatia are the implied subject of verbs.

---

20. Schreiner, *Galatians*, 23.
21. Similarly, Moo, *Galatians*, s.vv. "Introduction to Galatians."
22. Similarly, Moo, *Galatians*, s.vv. "Introduction to Galatians."
23. This leads to an earlier date (late 40s) for the writing of Galatians (Moo, *Galatians*, s.vv. "Introduction to Galatians").
24. Schreiner, *Galatians*, 28–29.

What insights can we gain at this high level? First, beyond an obvious abundance of second-person plural references to the Galatians, noun and first-person plural references (inclusive of Paul and the audience) fill the letter. This consistency in addressee confirms that Galatians belongs among the letters Paul wrote to churches. Second, the churches of Galatia appear to be significant participants throughout the letter. The notable exception is 1:13—2:21, where Paul cites examples from his life and ministry that support the divine nature of his calling and message. Third, notwithstanding "O foolish Galatians" in 3:1, Paul generally avoids completely equating his audience with having become people who fully embrace the errors warned against. Instead, he addresses his warning to "those who want to be under the law" (οἱ ὑπὸ νόμον θέλοντες [4:21]) and "as many as are justified by the law" (οἵτινες ἐν νόμῳ δικαιοῦσθε [5:4]).

Table 6: The Churches of Galatia as a Participant in the Overall Letter		
Noun References	Pronoun References	Implied Subject of Verbs
1:2 (ταῖς ἐκκλησίαις τῆς Γαλατίας)	1:3 (2x), 4 (3x), 6, 7, 8 (2x), 9	1:6, 9
1:11 (ἀδελφοί)	1:11, 20; 2:4 (2x), 5	1:13; 2:4
3:1 (Ὦ ἀνόητοι Γαλάται)	3:1 (2x), 2, 5 (2x), 13 (2x)	3:2, 3 (3x), 4, 7, 14
3:15 (Ἀδελφοί)	3:24, 26, 27	3:23 (2x), 24, 25
3:27 (ὅσοι εἰς Χριστὸν ἐβαπτίσθητε)	3:28, 29; 4:3, 6, 11 (2x)	3:29; 4:3, 5, 6, 7, 8 (2x), 9 (5x), 10
4:12 (ἀδελφοί)	4:12 (2x), 13, 14, 15 (3x), 16 (2x), 17 (2x), 18	4:12 (2x), 13, 14 (3x), 15 (2x), 17, 18
4:19 (τέκνα μου)	4:19 (2x), 20 (2x)	4:21 (2x)
4:21 (οἱ ὑπὸ νόμον θέλοντες)	4:26	4:21 (2x)
4:28 (ἀδελφοί)	4:28	
4:31 (ἀδελφοί)	5:1, 2 (2x), 4, 5, 7, 8, 10 (2x)	4:31; 5:1 (2x), 2, 7, 10
5:4 (οἵτινες ἐν νόμῳ δικαιοῦσθε)[25]		5:4

---

25. This is linked to παντὶ ἀνθρώπῳ περιτεμνομένῳ (every man who is circumcised [5:3]). Paul also partially distances the churches of Galatia from this error by stressing that they actually agree with him against it (5:5, 10).

5:11 (ἀδελφοί)	5:12, 13	
5:13 (ἀδελφοί)	5:13, 15 (2x), 21, 26 (2x)	5:13, 15 (4x), 16 (2x), 17 (2x), 18 (2x), 25 (2x), 26 (3x)
6:1 (Ἀδελφοί)	6:1	
6:1 (οἱ πνευματικοί)	6:1 (2x), 2, 11, 12, 13 (2x), 14, 18 (2x)	6:1, 2 (2x), 7, 9 (4x), 10 (2x), 11
6:18 (ἀδελφοί)		

When he formerly preached the gospel to them, they had received him as if an angel of God or even Christ Jesus himself had appeared to proclaim the good news to them. Their regard for Paul was so great that were it possible, they would have plucked out their own eyes and given them to him. Even Paul's illness (which in some sense created the occasion for him to preach to them) did not prevent them from accepting Paul as a divine messenger. However, they had changed their mind about Paul. Paul now wondered what happened to their earlier pronouncement of blessing that Paul was a person specially favored by God (4:13–15). Nevertheless, Paul still held a deep affection for them. He gave birth to them, and they are his dear children (4:19). He still often addressed them as brothers and sisters (1:11; 3:15; 4:12, 28, 31; 5:11, 13; 6:1, 18) in the household of faith. To avoid duplication, I will address further aspects of Paul's portrayal of his recipients when treating the letter's occasion in 1:6–7.

B. Grace and Peace Come from Jesus Rescuing Us from the Present Evil Age (1:3–5)

A prayer wish fills the spot of the conventional greeting in all of Paul's letters (Rom 1:7; 1 Cor 1:3; 2 Cor 1:2; Gal 1:3; Eph 1:2; Phil 1:2; Col 1:2; 1 Thess 1:1; 2 Thess 1:2; 1 Tim 1:2; 2 Tim 1:2; Titus 1:4; Phlm 1:3). However, Paul does not simply wish his audience grace and peace from God and Jesus in Gal 1:3 like he usually does.[26] Galatians 1:4 stands out as an unprecedented

---

26. The most common form is χάρις ὑμῖν καὶ εἰρήνη ἀπὸ θεοῦ πατρὸς ἡμῶν καὶ κυρίου Ἰησοῦ Χριστοῦ (Rom 1:7; 1 Cor 1:3; 2 Cor 1:2; Gal 1:3; Eph 1:2; Phil 1:2; 2 Thess 1:2; and Phlm 1:3). Another less common variant adds "mercy" in between "grace" and "peace" (χάρις ἔλεος εἰρήνη ἀπὸ θεοῦ πατρὸς καὶ Χριστοῦ Ἰησοῦ τοῦ κυρίου ἡμῶν [1 Tim 1:2; 2 Tim 1:2; Titus 1:4]). Col 1:2 omits Jesus (χάρις ὑμῖν καὶ εἰρήνη ἀπὸ θεοῦ πατρὸς ἡμῶν). 1 Thess 1:1 simply has χάρις ὑμῖν καὶ εἰρήνη.

extended portrait, where Paul painstakingly depicts how he wants his audience to view God and Jesus.[27]

Upon noticing the expanded description in the prayer wish, Paul's extra comments about God and Jesus when relating his apostleship to them in Gal 1:1 also becomes more conspicuous. Let us circle back to them before we return to discuss the prayer wish. Paul unexpectedly reversed his typical pattern of placing God the Father as the center of attention and relating Jesus to God. In every other case where Paul mentions both the Father and the Son, the Father is consistently named first. In Gal 1:1, Jesus comes first and the Father second. The Father also receives a more extended description that relates him to Jesus.[28] Specifically, God the Father is portrayed as raising Jesus from the dead (1:1). This is consistent with how Paul later mentions receiving his gospel through Jesus first (1:12) before connecting his calling to the Father (1:15–16).

The reversal of the typical pattern and extended descriptions appear to prepare the way to correct the readers' mental representation of Jesus's role and God's relation to Jesus: Jesus is central, and God himself affirmed this by raising him from the dead. However, I do not detect the topic of Jesus's resurrection later in the letter. This appears to be a shared belief in the background (unlike in 1 Corinthians, where Jesus's bodily resurrection is apparently up for debate). Likewise, Jesus as the Christ and Lord does not require argumentation or explanation. First, Paul's readers likely have sufficient background knowledge not to need clarification. Second, Paul can assume these shared beliefs as background he can rely on to support the areas that do need further explanation or correction.

So, what things do the readers still need to learn about Jesus? The answer comes from observing what aspects of Paul's depiction of Jesus are taken up later in the letter. After anchoring God to Jesus, Paul reverts to his usual pattern in the prayer wish in vv. 3–4.[29] As previously noted, Paul departs from his usual practice in his prayer wishes and further expands on his portrayal of God and Jesus within the wish (1:4). Specifically, Paul defines Jesus in relation to God as having obeyed him and given himself (δόντος ἑαυτὸν) for[30] our sins to rescue us from this present evil age. In this

---

27. Runge explains this as thematic highlighting, where the writer wants you to "think about a particular participant in a particular way" (*Discourse Grammar*, 322–23).

28. Runge, *Galatians*, Gal 1:1–5.

29. It is uncertain whether the pronoun ἡμῶν ("our") modifies God or Lord. See Moo, *Galatians*, s.vv. "Prescript" (Gal 1:1–5), "Additional Note." This textual variant does not result in a significant difference in interpretation.

30. It is uncertain whether the preposition ὑπέρ or περί should be read here. See Moo, *Galatians*, s.vv. "Prescript" (Gal 1:1–5), "Additional Note." This textual variant

portrayal, Jesus did the rescuing. However, God is to receive glory for ages of ages (1:5) for conceiving this rescue and sending Jesus to carry it out.[31] True grace and peace come from this good news and not any other.

Jesus's giving of himself (παραδόντος ἑαυτὸν) is emphasized again in 2:20 and linked with his death in 2:21. In comparison with Jesus's death, it seems that the purpose of his death (i.e., to enact God's rescue plan) receives relatively more attention. To look ahead, Paul develops different aspects of this rescue plan in the rest of this letter. First, he underscores that this rescue plan originated from God's will. Rejecting it is tantamount to rejecting God's grace (2:21). In the fullness of time (i.e., the time God appointed [4:2]), God sent Jesus (4:4). Second, while Paul does not define what he means by "this present evil age" here, he will delve into multiple aspects of what is involved. Later parts of the letter indicate that rescue from this present evil age includes dying to the law of Moses (2:19–21), being redeemed from the curse of the law (3:10–14), no longer being under the custody of the law (3:23–25), being redeemed from enslavement to the law and other elementary principles of the world, which include idols (4:1–11), and having crucified the flesh with its passions and desires (5:16–26). Even divisive religious, social, and sexual pairs of opposites are no longer relevant in light of the new oneness of God's people in Christ (3:26–29). In effect, the world has been crucified as far as believers are concerned, and believers have been crucified as far as the world is concerned (6:14). Believers are rescued from the present evil age (which corresponds to their death to the world) into the new creation (6:15).[32] Given the prominence of this topic throughout the letter, Paul appears to lay the foundation for highlighting Jesus's obedient sacrifice to rescue us from this present evil age as at the heart of his message in this letter (1:4).[33]

In this chapter, we have seen how Paul sets the scene in the letter opening, including the participants and their interpersonal roles. He lays foundational support for his overall message by reminding his audience that he speaks with divine authority and that Jesus's and God's purpose is to rescue them from this present evil age. In the next chapter, we will look at how Paul dives right into the letter's occasion: to rebuke and change perceptions. The rebuke (1:6-9) is followed by support (1:10—2:21), together forming the first round of rebuke with extended support.

---

does not result in a significant difference in interpretation.

31. DeSilva notes that the Greek idiom conceives of this "forever" as a sequence of "ages." While the meaning is "forever and ever," the juxtaposition of the Greek word αἰών in "this present evil age" and "the ages of ages" may also contrast God's true purpose for all the ages against the present evil age (*Galatians*, 121).

32. Moo, *Galatians*, s.vv. "Prescript" (Gal 1:1–5).

33. DeSilva, *Galatians*, 112.

GALATIANS 1:6—2:21

OUTLINE

I. Letter Opening (1:1–5)

II. First Round of Rebuke, Backed by Extended Support (1:6—2:21)

    A. Rebuke and Changing Perceptions (1:6–9)

    B. Paul Is a Servant of Christ and Proclaims a Divine Rather Than Human Gospel (1:10—2:21)

II. FIRST ROUND OF REBUKE, BACKED BY EXTENDED SUPPORT (1:6—2:21)

TABLE 7 BELOW PROVIDES an overview of the higher-level discourse flow of 1:6—2:21. It is the first of many I will use to illustrate the flow of the text's higher-level units. The "Connector" column lists the conjunctions and other grammatical or lexical features that connect a clause or series of clauses to other clauses. The "At" column records the verse reference for where the Connector occurs. Because connectors connect clauses before and after it, I will use two separate columns to track the before and after parties. The "Connects" column indicates the clauses that come after the connector. The "With" column notes the clauses that come before the connector. The "Function" column defines how the "Connector" connects the clauses after with the clauses before. I will offer both overview tables of larger units and more detailed tables covering smaller units. Tables that cover a smaller unit (like table 8, later below) will provide a relatively more complete account. To keep the tables from becoming too large and complicated, overview tables (like table 7 below) will group clauses that serve a larger function together.[1]

Table 7: Overview of the Flow of 1:6—2:21				
Connector	At	Connects	With	Function
None	1:6			Major break (starts first-round rebuke)
γάρ	1:10	1:10—2:21	1:6–9	Supports
γάρ	1:11	1:11—2:21	1:10	Supports
γάρ	1:12	1:12—2:21	1:11	Supports
γάρ	1:13	1:13—2:21	1:12	Supports (first of five)
ἔπειτα	1:18	1:18–20	1:12–17	Supports (second of five)
ἔπειτα	1:21	1:21–24	1:12–20	Supports (third of five)
ἔπειτα	2:1	2:1–10	1:12–24	Supports (fourth of five)
Ὅτε δὲ	2:11	2:11–21	1:12—2:10	Supports (fifth of five)

Galatians 1:6—2:21 is unified as a unit in support of Paul's first round of rebuke. Galatians 1:6–9 expresses the letter's occasion, which involves rebuking and changing perceptions. Paul's claims in 1:10–12 that he is a servant of Christ (who seeks approval from God rather than humans) and proclaims a divine rather than human gospel support this rebuke-focused paragraph. The autobiographical material of 1:13—2:21, in turn, supports Paul's claims in 1:10–12.[2] Paul's confrontation with Peter (2:11–21) also supports the condemnation of those who proclaim "a gospel contrary to what you received" (1:9).[3]

---

1. To keep these tables easier to digest, I will generally group coordinated clauses together (because they connect to other clauses in the same way) and leave out many subordinate clauses (discussing them only in my comments).

2. ἔπειτα in 1:18, 21; 2:1 introduces three further events in chronological sequence after the event 1:13–17 that supports 1:10–12. Ὅτε δὲ in 2:11 introduces a fourth supportive incident.

3. This is in broad agreement (with some differences in details) with Levinsohn, "Galatians," 306.

A. Rebuke and Changing Perceptions (1:6–9)

Table 8 below provides an overview of the discourse flow of 1:6–9. Since it covers a smaller unit than table 7 above, it offers a relatively more complete accounting of how the clauses fit together.[4]

Table 8: The Flow of 1:6–9				
Connector	At	Connects	With	Function
None	1:6			Major break (starts first-round rebuke)
Relative clause	1:7a	1:7a	1:6	Redefines (by negative description)
εἰ μή	1:7b	1:7b	1:7a	Exception
ἀλλά	1:8	1:8–9	1:6–7	Corrects (in contrast)
Closely related concept	1:9	1:9	1:8	Reinforces (by restatement)

Looking at the table, the mainline of 1:6–9 stands out: In 1:6, Paul offers his frank appraisal, expressing astonishment that the Galatians are quickly deserting the gospel he preached (1:6).[5] He offers his evaluation to get his audience to share it.[6] Galatians 1:7–9 reinforces Paul's astonishment by elaborating on the severity of deserting the gospel. Specifically, his further elaborations (i.e., the relative and exceptive clauses) in 1:7 explain the validity of his evaluation. Furthermore, the ἀλλά that connects 1:8–9 to 1:6–7 contrasts Paul's reaction (curse the false teachers) with the Galatians' response to the false gospel (follow their teaching). Paul's stance (1:8–9) serves as a corrective to their response, which implies that they should share Paul's evaluation. So, within the discourse flow, 1:6–9 is a rebuke-focused paragraph that heads up the first round of rebuke in 1:6—2:21.

How does this paragraph compare to how Paul usually continues his letters after the opening? Well, Paul typically includes a prayer of thanksgiving following the opening greeting. In these thanksgivings, Paul thanks

---

4. To make these tables easier to digest, grouping coordinated clauses together and leaving out many subordinate clauses is still often necessary.

5. Both the main verb introducing the appraisal (Θαυμάζω) and the main verb of the appraisal content (μετατίθεσθε) are present tense–form verbs (i.e., imperfective aspect), as expected for the mainline for nonnarrative.

6. As Callow notes, with an expressive utterance, "the speaker expresses his opinions not to get the hearer to believe them, but to get him to share them" (*Man and Message* 7.3.3.3, "Expressives in Relation to the Hearer").

God for specific aspects of the recipients' faith or behavior, for example, "I thank my God . . . for all of you" (Rom 1:8). They typically introduce significant themes that Paul later elaborates on in the letter.[7] In Galatians, Paul instead opens with an expression of astonishment and disbelief (1:6–7).[8] Subsequently, rather than offering a prayer, a curse is pronounced (1:8–9). While the Galatian churches might or might not have been familiar with Paul's usual practice in his other letters,[9] they cannot mistake Paul's intent here. They would immediately recognize that Paul is rebuking them for their actions during his absence.[10] In addition, the heavy concentration of the related words "gospel" (εὐαγγέλιον [vv. 6, 7]) and "proclaim the gospel" (εὐαγγελίζω [vv. 8 (2x), 9]) in this section highlight the heart of the dispute. (Note: I separated 1:6–9 into three subsections below to facilitate discussing the role of opponents separately. After this exception, in the rest of this commentary, the headings and subheadings will almost always correspond to meaningful paragraphs and paragraph groups.)[11]

1. Undermining the "Other Gospel" (1:6–7)

Even though Paul gets right to the point, it is still striking how skillfully he reshapes the Galatians' understanding. He is well prepared to challenge the Galatians' beliefs and practices.

First, Paul underscores the swiftness of their shift by placing "how quickly" before (rather than its default position after) the verb ("turned away"). He expresses astonishment not only at their turning away but also at how rapidly they have done so. Paul's emphasis on their rapid departure from the gospel adds poignancy to his rebuke.

---

7. See O'Brien, *Introductory Thanksgivings*; Jervis, *Purpose of Romans*, 86–109.

8. As Yoon notes, 1:5 ending with ἀμήν (Amen) and the lack of a conjunction linking 1:6 to 1:5 signal the end of the letter opening and the beginning of a new section here (*Discourse Analysis of Galatians*, 143).

9. DeSilva, *Galatians*, 123. This depends on whether or not Galatians is an early letter and whether or not other letters from Paul were already in wide circulation. As Van Voorst notes, the papyrology evidence shows that expressions of thanksgiving, while attested, were not customary in Hellenistic letters ("No Thanksgiving Period," 166). So, the Galatians would not have expected a thanksgiving section based on common letter-writing practices alone. To clarify, given that I believe that Galatians is an early letter (if not the first), I am not arguing that the Galatians know Paul's customary practice either. It is really for later interpreters like us that this difference becomes more apparent by comparison.

10. Moo, *Galatians*, s.vv. "Rebuke: The Occasion of the Letter" (Gal 1:6–10).

11. I will also discuss the supporting premises in 1:10 and 1:11–12 separately, even though they belong together.

Second, Paul metaphorically portrays the Galatians' decisions as a journey from one place to another. He describes the gospel he preached and the new one they have adopted as if they are locations on a map. The Galatians changed locations by "turning away from the one who called you in the grace of Christ to another gospel" (1:6–7).[12]

Third, Paul underscores the gravity of the situation by portraying the Galatians as turning away from God rather than simply turning away from the gospel. Indeed, by portraying God as "the one who called you in the grace of Christ" instead of a generic term like simply "God," the Galatians' acceptance of the rival teachers' message is fully exposed as a rejection of their divine benefactor's gracious invitation.[13]

Fourth, "in the grace of Christ" situates the calling the Galatians received from God as another figurative place. "Called you in the grace of Christ"[14] is linked to God's call and the gospel of Christ.[15] As a result, deserting the gospel Paul preached to another so-called gospel is tantamount to abandoning God's grace revealed in the gospel of Christ.[16]

Fifth, Paul uses two related verbs that could indicate a state change in 1:6 and 1:7.[17] In so doing, the Galatians' "turning away" (μετατίθημι) from God and the troublemakers' "distorting" (μεταστρέφω) of the gospel of Christ is linked more closely. The source of the turning away can be traced to prior distortion of the gospel.

Sixth, Paul employs a rhetorical tactic to contrast his gospel more strongly with the other so-called gospel. In 1:6, he portrays the Galatians as moving toward "another gospel" in their departure from the one who called them. However, he immediately contradicts this in v. 7 by using a relative clause to redefine it as not a gospel at all. Indeed, the "other gospel" is not merely a different, acceptable approach. It irreconcilably contradicts the gospel of Christ. Along the way, Paul uses an exception clause to complete his redefinition of the competing message. It is another so-called gospel

---

12. Runge, *Galatians*, Gal 1:6–10.

13. DeSilva, *Galatians*, 125.

14. "Christ" is omitted in some important manuscripts. However, it has strong manuscript support otherwise, which favors its inclusion. See also Moo, *Galatians*, s.vv. "Rebuke: The Occasion of the Letter" (Gal 1:6–10).

15. In this context, "grace" may recall Paul's grace wish in 1:3, which comes from the Lord Jesus Christ, who gave himself for Paul's and his audience's sins to enact God's rescue plan. It links to Paul's warning that "you have fallen from grace" in 5:4. Moo, *Galatians*, s.vv. "Rebuke: The Occasion of the Letter" (Gal 1:6–10).

16. Runge, *Galatians*, Gal 1:6–10.

17. Both words are grouped together under domain 13.64, "μεταστρέφω; μετατρέπω; περιτρέπω; μετατίθημι; μεθίστημι," L&N 1:155.

only in the sense of serving the purposes of those who are trying to confuse the Galatian churches and want to distort the gospel of Christ.[18]

Paul's extremely negative evaluation of how quickly the Galatians had turned to another false gospel (1:6–7) is just a start. Subsequent rounds of rebuke use a mixture of rhetorical questions and unfavorable appraisals of the Galatians' actions to rebuke and change perceptions. Throughout the letter, Paul crafts a careful appeal comprised of multiple rounds of rebuke in this way, supported by extended exposition. Table 9 below shows only the second-person plural references to the churches of Galatia. Besides the extended exhortations in 5:16—6:10 and the letter closing in 6:11-18, the places with high concentrations of second-person plural references generally correspond to the rebuke-focused paragraphs within Paul's four rounds of rebuke.[19]

The second round of rebuke reveals Paul's unfavorable assessment of the Galatians as foolish and challenges them with a series of rhetorical questions (3:1–5). The third round begins with a summary of all they already agree with and have experienced (pointing back to what was previously spelled out in 3:7—4:7) in a then-now contrast to rhetorically challenge their return to weak and poor elements (4:8–9). Paul's expression of fear about whether his ministry to them had been in vain also reveals his adverse appraisal of the situation (4:11). He also rhetorically challenges the Galatian churches to rethink their unfavorable change in opinion of Paul and to recognize that he has not become their enemy by speaking the truth to them (4:15–16). His great concern for them and inability to change his tone further signal his adverse assessment (4:20). The fourth round issues a rhetorical challenge to the Galatians for not obeying the truth (5:7). It is accompanied by a strongly negative evaluation of the scenario of receiving circumcision (5:2–4) as well as of the false message and false messengers (5:8–12).

---

18. Similarly, Runge, *Galatians*, Gal 1:6–10.

19. I omitted the noun references from the table because they are less relevant to the question of high-concentration chain interaction. For your convenience, the noun references from table 6 are reproduced here: 1:2 (ταῖς ἐκκλησίαις τῆς Γαλατίας), 11 (ἀδελφοί); 3:1 (Ὦ ἀνόητοι Γαλάται), 15 (Ἀδελφοί), 27 (ὅσοι εἰς Χριστὸν ἐβαπτίσθητε); 4:12 (ἀδελφοί), 19 (τέκνα μου), 21 (οἱ ὑπὸ νόμον θέλοντες), 28 (ἀδελφοί), 31 (ἀδελφοί); 5:4 (οἵτινες ἐν νόμῳ δικαιοῦσθε), 11 (ἀδελφοί), 13 (ἀδελφοί); 6:1 (Ἀδελφοί), 1 (οἱ πνευματικοὶ), 18 (ἀδελφοί).

GALATIANS 1:6—2:21

Table 9: Second-Person Plural References to the Churches of Galatia

Pronoun References	Implied Subject of Verbs	Rebuke-Focused Paragraphs
1:3, 6, 7, 8 (2x), 9	1:6, 9	1:6–9 (first round)
1:11, 20; 2:5	1:13	
3:1 (2x), 2, 5 (2x)	3:2, 3 (3x), 4, 7	3:1–5 (second round)
3:26, 27, 28, 29	3:29	
4:11 (2x), 12 (2x), 13, 14, 15 (3x), 16 (2x), 17 (2x), 18, 19 (2x), 20 (2x)	4:6, 7, 8 (2x), 9 (5x), 10, 12 (2x), 13, 14 (3x), 15 (2x), 17, 18	4:8–20 (third round)
4:28	4:21 (4x)	
5:2 (2x), 4, 7, 8, 10 (2x), 12	5:1 (2x), 2, 4, 7, 10	5:2–12 (fourth round)
5:13 (2x), 15 (2x), 21; 6:1 (3x), 2	5:13, 15 (4x), 16 (2x), 17 (2x), 18 (2x); 6:1, 2 (2x), 7	
6:11, 12, 13 (2x), 18	6:11	

Paul's perplexity at how to deal with the Galatians does not extend to those leading them astray. He minces no words about his opponents who brought this other so-called gospel. He undermines their credibility by characterizing them as "those who are confusing you and who want to distort the gospel of Christ." Their so-called other gospel is really no gospel at all (1:7). The Galatian churches obviously would not want to side with the wrong camp. Table 10 shows the references to Paul's opponents in Galatia.

Table 10: Paul's Opponents in Galatia as a Participant in the Overall Letter

Noun References	Pronoun References	Implied Subject of Verbs
1:7 (οἱ ταράσσοντες ὑμᾶς καὶ θέλοντες μεταστρέψαι τὸ εὐαγγέλιον τοῦ Χριστοῦ)	4:17	4:17 (3x)
5:10 (ὁ ταράσσων ὑμᾶς)		5:10
5:12 (οἱ ἀναστατοῦντες ὑμᾶς)		
6:12 (Ὅσοι θέλουσιν εὐπροσωπῆσαι ἐν σαρκί)	6:12	
6:13 (οἱ περιτεμνόμενοι)	6:13	6:13 (2x)

Even though Paul rhetorically asked, "Who has bewitched you?" in 3:1 and "Who hindered you?" in 5:7, he was not interested in discovering their identity. In both instances, the implication is that no one could legitimately do these things. No matter who they are, whoever confuses the Galatians will bear their judgment (5:10). Paul will further portray his rivals as selfishly trying to gain the Galatians' slavish allegiance (4:17). They are a corrupting influence (5:9) that hinders the Galatians from obeying the truth (5:7). Their message did not come from God (5:8). He even goes so far as to wish that these who are troubling the Galatians would castrate themselves (5:12). We learn that they are trying to force the Galatians to be circumcised so that they can boast in the Galatians' circumcised flesh. Their real motive was to avoid persecution, which having their gentile followers circumcised accomplished (6:12–13).[20]

2. Curse Pronouncement (1:8–9)

Not only is the other "so-called" gospel not a gospel at all, but Paul also pronounces a curse on anyone who proclaims any so-called gospel to the Galatians[21] other than the gospel of Christ Paul had previously proclaimed to them.[22] At first glance, the function of the conjunction ἀλλά is unclear. This is because it is apparently connected to Paul's expressed negative evaluation. However, the ἀλλά can be read as connected to the content for which Paul expressed disapproval, i.e., the Galatians' response to the false gospel. Read in this way, the ἀλλά connects 1:8–9 to 1:6–7 to contrast Paul's stance towards the false gospel with the Galatians' response. Instead of accepting it, Paul condemns it firmly with a curse.[23] Paul's reaction thus serves as a

---

20. Barclay has shown how treacherous it is to try to reconstruct the situation with just one side of the conversation ("Mirror-Reading a Polemical Letter"). However, he still argued that it is necessary. I tend to agree instead with Hardin ("Galatians 1–2 Without a Mirror") that mirror reading is not needed. I will rely on explicit statements and avoid making too many inferences. On preferring explicit statements over inferences, see Silva, *Interpreting Galatians*, 104–8.

21. It is uncertain whether to read the pronoun ὑμῖν (you) or to omit it. See Moo, *Galatians*, s.vv. "Rebuke: The Occasion of the Letter" (Gal 1:6–10). It makes no significant difference in interpretation.

22. Similarly, Runge, *Galatians*, Gal 1:6–10.

23. Pronouncing a thing or a person ἀνάθεμα places them under God's curse or wrath and, therefore, set apart for destruction. See Moo, *Galatians*, s.vv. "Rebuke: The Occasion of the Letter" (Gal 1:6–10). Arichea and Nida observe that it is "a petition to God that the person referred to may be deprived of God's favor and be the object instead of his condemnation" (*Handbook on Galatians*, 14).

corrective to their response. They should have responded like Paul rather than turning away from the true gospel to follow a false one.²⁴

First, Paul posits a hypothetical scenario in v. 8 where the unlikeliest of characters were to preach a different gospel.²⁵ Paul would naturally be the furthest person one could imagine contradicting his own message. Angels from heaven would presumably be reliable messengers for God. If this scenario were to happen somehow, not even he (or other Christians with him)²⁶ or an angel from heaven could escape condemnation. By including both himself and heavenly angels, Paul effectively excludes any source that might claim divine authority to contradict the existing gospel.²⁷

Second, Paul emphatically reiterates in v. 9 that anyone who proclaims a gospel other than what the Galatian churches have previously received should be cursed. ὡς προειρήκαμεν καὶ ἄρτι πάλιν λέγω (as we have already said, so now I say again) could refer to what was said in v. 8 or on a previous occasion. This comment draws extra attention to his restated curse pronouncement.²⁸ Given that he had just mentioned previous preaching in warning against receiving anyone preaching a gospel other than "what we preached to you" in v. 8, I think it also refers to a past occasion when Paul and his colleagues preached to the Galatian churches. As for the actual curse, Paul repeats ἀνάθεμα ἔστω,²⁹ but generic "anyone" replaces Paul or an angel from heaven in the posited scenario. The perspective also shifts from what Paul and his colleagues preached to the Galatians to what the Galatians received (which refers to the same gospel). These lexical and conceptual connections further underscore Paul's condemnation of any potential contradiction of the gospel. Paul poses a less hypothetical scenario,

---

24. Besides contrast, in general, ἀλλά "provides a corrective to whatever it stands in contrast with in the preceding context" (Runge, *Discourse Grammar*, 93). As Runge notes elsewhere, 1:8–9 "sharply contrasts the Galatian believers' response to this new adaptation of the gospel with how they ought to have responded" (*Galatians*, Gal 1:6–10).

25. The sense in English is "even if" something so unimaginable were to happen, using a third-class conditional with ἐάν plus a subjunctive verb together with καί (Nicolle, "Conditionals in Galatians," 91).

26. Paul uses an inclusive "we," which probably includes the brothers and sisters with him in v. 2.

27. Schreiner, *Galatians*, 87.

28. Runge, *Galatians*, Gal 1:6–10. The perfect tense verb (stative aspect) of προειρήκαμεν is likewise noteworthy, adding prominence to Paul's curse that it introduces.

29. Present active imperative in both cases.

with a conditional clause inviting readers to consider whether the condition is fulfilled. He likely wants his readers to see that this curse applies to the opponents who proclaim another gospel.[30] After all, he has already stated that these opponents were trying to turn the Galatian believers away to a different gospel (v. 6).[31]

B. Paul Is a Servant of Christ and Proclaims a Divine Rather Than Human Gospel (1:10—2:21)

Next, Paul begins a lengthy section supporting his rebuke and attempting to change his audience's perceptions (1:10—2:21).[32] Even though it is made up entirely of support, I gave this section a separate heading to highlight its nature as extended support. Please refer to table 7, "Overview of the Flow of 1:6—2:21," for a visual representation.

Paul begins by asking two rhetorical questions: "Am I still trying to win the approval of human beings or of God? Or am I trying to please people?" How do these questions fit into the discourse? Interpreters differ. To help solve this puzzle, it should be noted that Paul uses γάρ in vv. 10, 11, 12, and 13. If all four are interpreted as signaling supporting explanations or reasons, the flow of Paul's argument would go as follows:

1. γάρ in v. 10 supports his strong opposition to the Galatians' turning away to a different gospel and his pronouncement of such a severe judgment (1:6-9). He does so because he tries to please God rather than humans as Christ's servant.

2. γάρ in v. 11 supports his assertion that he is a God-pleaser rather than a human-pleaser as Christ's servant (1:10) by clarifying that the gospel he preached is not of human origin.

3. γάρ in v. 12 supports the nonhuman origin of his gospel (1:11) by stating that he received it by the revelation of Jesus Christ and not from any human source.

---

30. Armitage, "Conditional Clause Exegesis," 383; Nicolle, "Conditionals in Galatians," 92-93.

31. DeSilva, *Galatians*, 128.

32. With some differences in how I account for the details, I basically agree with Levinsohn that the autobiographical material of 1:13-2:10 supports the declarations of 1:11-12, while the account of this confrontation with Peter (2:11-21) supports the condemnation of those who proclaim "a gospel contrary to what you received" (1:9), as well as showing that Paul was not seeking "human approval," but "God's approval" (1:10) (Levinsohn, "Galatians," 306).

4. γάρ in v. 13 supports his assertion that he received his gospel by divine revelation and not from any human source (1:12) with a selective recounting of key events in his life (1:13—2:21), starting with his persecution of the church.[33]

In this reading, 1:13—2:21 would support 1:12 directly. However, because it lies at the bottom of four support layers, it indirectly supports all of 1:6-12 (because 1:10, the first layer of support, supports 1:6-9). Likewise, each layer above 1:13—2:21 supports all the layers above it.

1. Transition to Support: Serving Christ as Justification for Opposing False Gospel (1:10)

Starting in v. 10, Paul transitions from directly rebuking the Galatians to supporting the strong opposition he expressed in 1:6-9. Table 11 zooms in on the flow within 1:10-12.

Table 11: The Flow of 1:10–12				
Connector	At	Connects	With	Function
γάρ	1:10a	1:10—2:21	1:6–9	Supports
Closely related concept	1:10c	1:10c	1:10a-b	Excludes (false hypothetical scenario)
γάρ	1:11	1:11—2:21	1:10	Supports
γάρ	1:12a	1:12—2:21	1:11	Supports
ἀλλά	1:12c	1:12c	1:12a-b	Corrects (in contrast)

As already noted above, the rhetorical questions ("For am I still trying to win the approval of human beings, or of God? Or am I trying to please people?") support Paul's strong opposition to the Galatians' defection to a different gospel and pronouncement of a curse (1:6-9).[34] The meaning of πείθω (persuade or win the approval) is uncertain.[35] However, even though

---

33. Levinsohn similarly sees each γάρ signaling that what follows strengthens the preceding material. Specifically, "the presence of γάρ in these verses indicates that the 'solemn curse' of 1:8, which is repeated in 1:9 to give it prominence, is strengthened by 1:10. In turn, 1:11 strengthens 1:10, 1:12 strengthens 1:11, and 1:13–2:14 (or 2:21 ...) strengthens 1:12" ("Discourse Analysis: Galatians," 120–21). See also Levinsohn, "Galatians," 305.

34. As Blight notes, this is perhaps the most common interpretation (*Exegetical Helps on Galatians*, Gal 1:10). One piece of evidence in support is ἄρτι (now), which can be seen as picking up the ἄρτι of v. 9 (Longenecker, *Galatians*, 18).

35. DeSilva, *Galatians*, 130–33.

Paul asked both whether he was trying to win the approval of humans and whether he was trying to please humans (1:10a–b), he only repeated the words "please humans" when posing the false scenario he wanted to deny (1:10c).

The implied answer to the first rhetorical question would seem to be: I am trying to win the approval of God. The implied answer to the second rhetorical question would, in turn, appear to be: I am not seeking to please human beings.[36] As noted above, instead of directly answering the rhetorical questions, Paul responds with a contrary-to-fact conditional statement: "If I were still trying to please people, I would not be a servant of Christ." By constructing a hypothetical scenario in which his pleasing people is portrayed as false (contrary to fact), Paul vehemently denies seeking people's approval and underscores his role as Christ's servant.[37] Notably, denying he was trying to please humans was a sufficient response to both rhetorical questions. This evidence suggests that "winning the approval of human beings" and "pleasing human beings" are closely related.

At the same time, Paul seems to indicate that his primary objective is to seek God's approval, which corresponds with his depiction of himself as a servant of Christ.[38] This fits with the notion of accountability to please God and Christ rather than humans implicit in Paul's prior emphasis on the divine origin of his apostleship. An "apostle" (ἀπόστολος) is a representative who is sent to convey a message or fulfill a specific task on behalf of another.[39] With apostleship from Christ and God rather than any human source (v. 1), Paul naturally aims to please God and Christ rather than humans.

---

36. Moo, *Galatians*, s.vv. "Rebuke: The Occasion of the Letter" (Gal 1:6–10). See also Verster, "Nonauthentic Questions in Galatians," 149–50.

37. Levinsohn suggests that Χριστοῦ (of Christ) may be placed before the noun it modifies (δοῦλος) for focused contrast with ἀνθρώποις (humans) in εἰ ἔτι ἀνθρώποις ἤρεσκον, Χριστοῦ δοῦλος οὐκ ἂν ἤμην (*Discourse Features* 4.5). In other words, the focused contrast is on pleasing or serving Christ rather than humans.

38. Schreiner, *Galatians*, 89. See also Hardin, "Galatians Without a Mirror," 298–99. I think that it is logically valid for Paul to use his not trying to please humans as a premise to support his claim to being Christ's servant (in disagreement with Nicolle, "Conditionals in Galatians," 94). One needs only to interpret Paul's premise as that trying to please humans rather than God is incompatible with being a servant of Christ. This can be done without implying that everyone who does not try to please humans is necessarily a servant of Christ. It can be a necessary but not sufficient condition. Paul's point is merely that if he were still trying to please people (which Paul explicitly denies with the contrary-to-fact conditional), he would not be a servant of Christ. Paul will continue to provide other reasons to support his assertions that he is not trying to please humans and that he is Christ's servant.

39. DeSilva, *Galatians*, 113–14.

2. Supporting Premises: Paul Proclaims a Divine Rather Than Human Gospel (1:11–12)

Are there any more reasons supporting Paul's claim to be serving Christ and not seeking the approval of human beings? As he made known to the Galatian churches, the gospel he proclaimed was not a human gospel (v. 11). Even though this is a supporting premise to Paul's claims in v. 10, the disclosure formula "I made known to you" and the direct address "brothers and sisters" highlights this premise.[40] Furthermore, "the gospel proclaimed by me" (τὸ εὐαγγέλιον τὸ εὐαγγελισθὲν ὑπ' ἐμοῦ) links back to 1:6-9 through the words "gospel" (εὐαγγέλιον, previously used in vv. 6 and 7) and "proclaim the gospel" (εὐαγγελίζω, previously used in vv. 8 [2x] and 9). The divine origin of the gospel Paul proclaims is thus signaled as the central premise of this extended supporting section (1:10—2:21).[41]

The fact that Paul had neither received his gospel from humans nor had been taught it, but had instead received it by the "revelation of Jesus Christ" (ἀποκαλύψεως Ἰησοῦ Χριστοῦ [v. 12]) further supports this premise. Strikingly, the way Paul speaks of the origin of his message closely parallels how he highlighted the origin of his apostolic authority in v. 1. Evidently, Paul saw the need to support his authority and message further.[42] In effect, Paul ties together and asserts the divine nature of both his message and his commission, emphasizing that they originate from Christ rather than human influence.[43] There is some uncertainty about what the "revelation of Jesus Christ" means. However, in light of 1:16 ("to reveal his Son to me" [ἀποκαλύψαι τὸν υἱὸν αὐτοῦ ἐν ἐμοί]), Paul most likely refers to God revealing Jesus to him on the Damascus road in both vv. 12 and 16.[44]

---

40. Levinsohn identifies these two factors and the fronting of τὸ εὐαγγέλιον τὸ εὐαγγελισθὲν ὑπ' ἐμοῦ as justifying a second-level division at 1:12 ("Discourse Analysis: Galatians," 121; *Galatians*, 305).

41. If the textual variant δέ is read instead of γάρ, v. 11 would signal a related but distinct point from v. 10 that goes further in some way (see Runge, *Discourse Grammar*, 31). This alternate reading would actually further strengthen the case for the divine origin of Paul's gospel as this section's main point.

42. What Paul provides fits under credential information that supports a speaker's right to give commands or opinions and expect them to be followed or shared. As Breeze notes, credential information "may draw attention to the authority the speaker or author has in the particular situation in which the exhortation is given, or it may appeal to a higher authority to reinforce one's own authority. It may also appeal to the knowledge and experience of the author" ("Hortatory Discourse in Ephesians" 2.3, "Bipartite and Tripartite Methods").

43. DeSilva, *Galatians*, 139–40.

44. Schreiner, *Galatians*, 97.

3. Supporting Evidence from Paul's Life and Ministry (1:13—2:21)

Table 12 below provides an overview of the discourse flow of 1:13—2:21.

Table 12: Overview of the Flow of 1:13—2:21				
Connector	At	Connects	With	Function
γάρ	1:13	1:13—2:21	1:12	Supports
ἔπειτα	1:18	1:18–20	1:12–17	Next (sequence)
ἔπειτα	1:21	1:21–24	1:12–20	Next (sequence)
ἔπειτα	2:1	2:1–10	1:12–24	Next (sequence)
Ὅτε δὲ	2:11	2:11–21	1:12—2:10	Next (distinct development)

Paul brings up evidence from his life and ministry to support his claim that he received his gospel not from humans, but by the revelation of Jesus Christ (vv. 11-12). The paragraphs that depict these events are primarily narrative in nature (with Paul's speech to Cephas embedded within the fifth narrative paragraph).[45] Three characteristics stand out in this section:

1. Focus on absence or presence in Jerusalem
2. Focus on absence or presence of interaction with the apostles in Jerusalem
3. Negative focus on things not done[46]

With γάρ in v. 13, Paul puts forth five sets of evidence from 1:13—2:21 as support.

1. 1:13-17: Paul's former conduct persecuting the church as a rising star in Judaism (1:13-14) did not prepare him to proclaim the gospel. Despite this, when (Ὅτε δὲ) Paul received his gospel by a revelation of Jesus Christ, he did not consult with others or seek affirmation from the apostles in Jerusalem (1:15-17).

2. 1:18-20: "Then" (ἔπειτα) Paul continued not to need affirmation from the apostles even when he did visit Jerusalem eventually.

---

45. Aorist tense-form verbs carry forward the story in line with expectations for narrative.

46. Moo, *Galatians*, s.vv. "How Paul Received and Defended the Gospel: Paul and the 'Pillars'" (Gal 1:11—2:14).

3. 1:21–24: "Then" (ἔπειτα) the churches in Judea, while not knowing Paul personally, affirmed the gospel he proclaimed by glorifying God for his conversion and preaching.

4. 2:1–10: "Then" (ἔπειτα) the leaders in Jerusalem, notably James, Cephas, and John, affirmed the gospel Paul proclaimed and added nothing to it.[47]

5. 2:11–21: Above all, when ("Οτε δὲ) Cephas was not straightforward about the truth of the gospel, Paul confronted and corrected him.[48]

A. DID NOT CONSULT WITH OTHERS OR SEEK AFFIRMATION AFTER CONVERSION (1:13–17)

Table 13: The Flow of 1:13–17				
Connector	At	Connects	With	Function
γὰρ	1:13	1:13—2:21	1:12	Supports
Ὅτε δὲ	1:15	1:15–17	1:13–14	Contrasts (after with before)
ἀλλ'	1:17b	1:17b–c	1:16c–17a	Corrects (in contrast)

First, Paul cites his prior life in Judaism and his encounter with the glorified Christ that turned his life around. It seems that Paul's past as a persecutor of the church was well known (e.g., 1 Cor 15:8–10; Phil 3:6; 1 Tim 1:13). Paul may even have told the Galatian churches the story personally as part of his proclamation of the gospel.[49] In any case, Paul starts by appealing to common ground—something they had previously heard.

Paul mentions two sets of characteristics from his former life in Judaism:

1. He persecuted the church intensely and tried to destroy it (v. 13).

---

47. Yoon notes the cohesive ties formed by the abundance of verbs of linear movement (domain 15, "Linear Movement," L&N 1:180–210) together with ἔπειτα at 1:18, 21; 2:1 (*Discourse Analysis of Galatians*, 146). On verbs of linear movement, note ἀνῆλθον, ἀπῆλθον, and ὑπέστρεψα (1:17), ἀνῆλθον (1:18), ἦλθον (1:21), and ἀνέβην (2:1, 2). To go beyond Yoon's observations, verbs of linear movement actually resume in 2:11 and 2:12 as well, but the participant changes from Paul to Peter and certain ones from James. Between 1:13—2:10, Paul's personal travels further support his contention in 1:15–17 that he received his gospel by a revelation of Jesus Christ and did not consult with others or seek affirmation from the apostles in Jerusalem.

48. Similarly, Parunak, "Dimensions of Discourse Structure," 224–25.

49. Fung, *Galatians*, 55.

2. Being exceedingly zealous in the practice of his ancestral traditions, he was a rising star, advancing beyond many of his Jewish contemporaries (v. 14).[50]

Interestingly, Paul reveals how his fervor for upholding his inherited Jewish traditions contributed to his advancement in Judaism. It may be no coincidence that Paul portrays things in this way. The Galatian churches were trying to blend those traditions with the gospel. If there was ever a time when Paul sought to please people and gain human approval, it was while he was still following the Jewish way of life and persecuting the church (v. 13).[51] Implicitly, it seems that the ancestral traditions are cast as human in origin in contrast to the divine gospel.

At the same time, Paul's life before Christ sets the scene for a contrast between pre-conversion ("former [ποτε] way of life in Judaism") and post-conversion ("but when" ["Οτε δὲ]). Nothing in Paul's pre-conversion life could account for the gospel he was now proclaiming, which provides helpful background to bolster its divine origin.[52] By contrast, the time when God was pleased to reveal his Son to him brings a related, new development in Paul's life.

By characterizing God as "the one who separated me from my mother's womb and called me through his grace" (ὁ ἀφορίσας με ἐκ κοιλίας μητρός μου καὶ καλέσας διὰ τῆς χάριτος αὐτοῦ) in v. 15,[53] Paul, first of all, connects himself to the Galatian churches as having been called by God in his grace (τοῦ καλέσαντος ὑμᾶς ἐν χάριτι Χριστοῦ [v. 6]). However, Paul also seems to associate himself with God's calling of Isaiah and Jeremiah as prophets while they were still in their mother's wombs (Isa 49:1; Jer 1:5). Like Isaiah and Jeremiah before him, Paul likewise was divinely appointed and set aside for a God-given task before birth (Rom 1:1).[54]

Paul's call can only be explained by God's will and good pleasure when God was "pleased to reveal his Son" to Paul. The verb "to reveal" (ἀποκαλύψαι) is related to the noun "revelation" (ἀποκαλύψεως) in v. 12 and likely recalls it. So, "by the revelation of Jesus Christ" in v. 12 and "reveal

---

50. In a context where the aorist tense forms carry the narrative, the imperfect tense verbs that describe Saul's past signal offline, nonevent information. See Runge, *Discourse Grammar*, 129–30.

51. Runge, *Galatians*, Gal 1:11–24.

52. George, *Galatians*, 113.

53. ὁ θεὸς is textually uncertain and probably should be omitted. "His Son" in v. 16 unmistakably identifies God as the referent. See also Moo, *Galatians*, s.vv. "Conversion and Early Travels" (Gal 1:13–17); Longenecker, *Galatians*, 30.

54. Schreiner, *Galatians*, 101.

his Son to me" in v. 16 likely refer to God revealing Jesus Christ to Paul on the Damascus road.[55] The purpose of God's call is that Paul might proclaim Christ among the gentiles (v. 16). The importance of this proclamation is underscored by how often this concept is repeated in a short span. "Proclaim him" (εὐαγγελίζωμαι αὐτὸν) links back to "the gospel proclaimed by me" (τὸ εὐαγγέλιον τὸ εὐαγγελισθὲν ὑπ' ἐμοῦ) in 1:11. These occurrences in turn recall previous mentions of the "gospel" (εὐαγγέλιον [1:6, 7]), and "proclaim the gospel" (εὐαγγελίζω [1:8 (2x), 9]).

With all the elaboration and the contrast between pre- and post-conversion, we must not lose track of Paul's main point in 1:15–17, namely that he did not immediately[56] consult with anyone[57] or go up[58] to Jerusalem to see those who were apostles before him.[59] Indeed, this is the main point of 1:13–17: Despite nothing in his religious background preparing him for the gospel he was now proclaiming, Paul did not need to consult or get affirmation from anyone because he received his gospel by God's direct revelation of Jesus (which by the way God had set Paul aside to do while he was still in his mother's womb).[60]

Paul acknowledges that some in Jerusalem became apostles before he did. However, by characterizing them as "those who were apostles before me" (τοὺς πρὸ ἐμοῦ ἀποστόλους), Paul subtly reiterates his own status as an apostle.[61] Instead of immediately consulting or seeking affirmation from the Jerusalem apostles (ἀλλ'), Paul went to Arabia and (καὶ) returned again to Damascus (1:17).[62] Paul's actions underscore his independence from the

---

55. Similarly Schreiner, *Galatians*, 100.

56. Paul's use of "immediately" (εὐθέως) probably reflects the fact that he would go on to mention that he did eventually visit the apostles in Jerusalem and consult other humans (1:18–20; 2:1–2). See also DeSilva, *Galatians*, 148–49; George, *Galatians*, 123.

57. "Flesh and blood" (σαρκὶ καὶ αἵματι) refers to human beings. Besides ties to Paul's points about the nonhuman origin of his gospel and his lack of need to gain the approval of or please humans (1:1, 11–12), this designation may also highlight humans as frail and mortal.

58. "Paul uses a typical verb for travel toward Jerusalem: to move toward Jerusalem from any compass direction is to 'go up,' reflecting the slight geographic, but significant ideological, elevation of the city on Mount Zion" (DeSilva, *Galatians*, 157).

59. Longenecker, *Galatians*, 30, 32.

60. Runge, *Galatians*, Gal 1:11–24.

61. DeSilva, *Galatians*, 157.

62. The mention of his return again to Damascus likely confirms that the reference to "God revealed his Son to me" in v. 16 refers to Paul's conversion on the Damascus road (see further Bruce, *Galatians*, 96). In this reading, "Galatians fills out the historical record by informing us that Paul, after spending some time in Damascus, traveled to Arabia, and then returned later to Damascus" (Schreiner, *Galatians*, 102).

apostles in Jerusalem or any other potential human authority.[63] This independence correspondingly supports his assertion that he received his gospel by the revelation of Jesus Christ.

B. Had Only Limited Interaction with Two Apostles on Eventual Visit (1:18–20)

Table 14: The Flow of 1:18–20				
Connector	At	Connects	With	Function
ἔπειτα	1:18	1:18–20	1:12–17	Next (sequence)
δέ	1:19a	1:19	1:18	Elaborates (rules out all apostles)
εἰ μή	1:19b	1:19b	1:19a	Exception (James, the Lord's brother)
δέ	1:20	1:20	1:18–19	Elaborates (and reinforces with an oath)

The next event ("then" [ἔπειτα]) happened three years later. Paul went up to Jerusalem to visit Cephas.[64] He stayed with Cephas for fifteen days (v. 18). Moreover (δέ), he did not see any of the other apostles, except for (εἰ μή) James, the brother of the Lord (v. 19).

The time frames mentioned are significant. Here, Paul concedes that he eventually visited the apostles in Jerusalem. However, this first visit did not happen until three years later. Furthermore, Paul stayed only fifteen days with Cephas. In addition, Paul draws attention to the fact that besides Cephas, he did not see any of the other apostles during this visit, except for James, the brother of Jesus.[65] This is the main point of 1:18–20. Furthermore, Paul adds the weight of an oath to his claims about the limits of his interaction with the apostles: "Now [δέ] about the things I am writing to you, look! Before God I swear that I am not lying" (v. 20).[66]

So, despite potential perceptions to the contrary (because he did end up visiting the apostles in Jerusalem), Paul remained independent from

---

63. Wiarda notes that Paul's main concern in 1:13–24 is to highlight distance from Jerusalem and not consulting human teachers ("Plot and Character," 240–41).

64. Some manuscripts read "Peter" (Πέτρον) instead of "Cephas" (Κηφᾶν). However, the manuscript evidence here favors Cephas. Moreover, Paul regularly uses the Aramaic name of the apostle Peter in his letter. In fact, Paul refers to this apostle as Peter only in Gal 2:7–8.

65. Runge, *Galatians*, Gal 1:11–24.

66. DeSilva, *Galatians*, 164. Paul uses oath formulas elsewhere to reinforce the truth of what he said (e.g., Rom 1:9; 9:1; 2 Cor 1:23; Phil 1:8; 1 Tim 2:7).

them. Again, events from Paul's life and ministry support his assertion that he received his gospel by the revelation of Jesus Christ.

C. Remained Absent from Jerusalem While Judean Churches Affirmed His Gospel from Afar (1:21–24)

Table 15: The Flow of 1:21-24				
Connector	At	Connects	With	Function
ἔπειτα	1:21	1:21–24	1:12–20	Next (sequence)
δὲ	1:22	1:22	1:21	Elaborates
μόνον δὲ	1:23	1:23–24	1:21–22	Elaborates an exception
καὶ	1:24	1:24	1:23	Associated (response)

"Then" (ἔπειτα), Paul went into the regions of Syria and Cilicia (v. 21).[67] Paul focuses on his absence from Jerusalem rather than providing details about his work in Syria and Cilicia. Moreover (δὲ), he "remained unknown by face among the Judean congregations that are in Christ" (v. 22).[68] In other words, he did not seek validation from other believers in Israel either, most of whom did not know him personally.[69] This is the main point of 1:21–24.

Nevertheless, there was an exception to this lack of knowledge. Paul was known by reputation. They had not seen him face to face, but (δὲ) had only (μόνον) heard about him: "But only they were hearing: the one who formerly used to persecute us is now proclaiming the faith that he was formerly trying to destroy" (v. 23). The way Paul recalls the language in vv. 13 and 16 is likely significant. The Judean churches had heard essentially the same story as the Galatian churches about Paul, the persecutor of the church, now proclaiming Christ.[70] In addition (καὶ), by noting that the Judean believers "were glorifying God because of me" (v. 24), Paul effectively produces them as witnesses to God's work in his call and apostleship.[71]

---

67. Paul's hometown Tarsus is in Cilicia. This account is consistent with Acts 11:25–26, which recounts that Barnabas found Paul in Tarsus and brought him to Syrian Antioch.

68. DeSilva, *Galatians*, 165.

69. Schreiner, *Galatians*, 112.

70. "Proclaiming the faith that he was once trying to destroy" (εὐαγγελίζεται τὴν πίστιν ἥν ποτε ἐπόρθει) links back to "proclaim him" (εὐαγγελίζωμαι αὐτὸν) in 1:16 (and also to 1:6, 7, 8 [2x], 9, 11 before it). It also links back to "I was persecuting the church of God and trying to destroy it" (ἐδίωκον τὴν ἐκκλησίαν τοῦ θεοῦ καὶ ἐπόρθουν αὐτήν) in 1:13.

71. DeSilva, *Galatians*, 168.

D. James, Cephas, and John Affirmed Paul's Gospel and Added Nothing to It (2:1–10)

Table 16: The Flow of 2:1–10				
Connector	At	Connects	With	Function
ἔπειτα	2:1	2:1–10	1:12–24	Next (sequence)
δέ (2x)[72]	2:2	2:2	2:1	Elaborates (on circumstances)
ἀλλά	2:3	2:3	2:1–2	Corrects (in contrast)
δέ[73]	2:4	2:4–5	2:1–3	Elaborates (on opponents)
Relative clause[74]	2:5	2:5	2:4	Describes (Paul's response)
δέ[75]	2:6a	2:6	2:1–5	Elaborates (on audience)
γάρ	2:6d	2:6d	2:6a–c	Supports
ἀλλὰ τοὐναντίον[76]	2:7	2:7–10	2:1–6	Corrects (in contrast)
μόνον	2:10a	2:10	2:7–9	Exception
Relative clause	2:10b	2:10b	2:10a	Redefines (exception in 2:10a)

"Then" (ἔπειτα), fourteen years later,[77] Paul went up "again" (πάλιν) to Jerusalem with Barnabas, taking along Titus also (2:1). Barnabas's presence leads to his receiving the right hand of fellowship along with Paul (2:9). Even more significantly, Titus's presence leads to his becoming a precedent for gentiles not being compelled to be circumcised (2:3). As previously noted, ἔπειτα here and in 1:18 and 1:21 links the four sets of evidence together.[78]

---

72. To keep the table more readable, I have grouped together two clauses associated together by καί and subsumed the negative purpose clause that is subordinate to the clause introduced by the second δέ.

73. I have grouped together two relative clauses that further describe the false brothers and our freedom respectively, as well as a purpose clause that reveals the false brothers' purpose.

74. I have grouped together a purpose clause that reveals Paul's purpose with the relative clause that describes Paul's resolute opposition to the false brothers.

75. I have grouped together a fronted incomplete clause and two parenthetical clauses in 2:6a–c.

76. The clauses grouped together here cannot be summarized well in a footnote. See my comments on these verses.

77. Note that it is uncertain whether this is fourteen years after Paul's encounter with the glorified Christ (1:15–17) or after his first visit to Jerusalem (1:18–20). See further Moo, *Galatians*, s.vv. "Date."

78. Schreiner, *Galatians*, 119.

"Again" refers back to the first visit to Jerusalem and makes this a subsequent visit.[79] Like in 1:18, the time frame is again noteworthy. Only fourteen years later did Paul interact significantly with the apostles on another visit to Jerusalem.

Paul uses a development marker (δέ) twice in v. 2 to slowly unpack the circumstances, processes, characters involved, and the purpose of this visit. He elaborates (δέ) that he "went up in response to a revelation."[80] And (καί) he proceeded to present the gospel he proclaimed among the gentiles[81] to "them."[82] Moreover, he clarified (δέ) that by "them" he meant "those who appear to be important" (τοῖς δοκοῦσιν).[83] He emphasized that this happened "privately" (κατ' ἰδίαν).[84] He also expressed the purpose of his actions: to prevent any possibility that he was running or had run in vain.

Paul uses running imagery, which he also employs elsewhere for his ministry (1 Cor 9:26; Phil 2:16) and for the Christian life (Gal 5:7). Why would he admit that his work in spreading the gospel would be futile if the apostles in Jerusalem disagreed with him on its content? The most plausible explanation lies in Paul's pragmatic approach to the situation. He was evaluating the potential consequences that could arise if the apostles did not share his views. Paul's gospel's validity was not in question as it came through divine revelation. If the apostles diverged from Paul's views, his work could unravel once the Jerusalem apostles' opinion reached the Pauline churches. So, while Paul did not require their endorsement to confirm

---

79. Runge, *Galatians*, Gal 2:1–10; Longenecker, *Galatians*, 45.

80. This revelation may correspond to the prophecy from Agabus in Acts 11:27–30.

81. "The gospel I proclaimed among the gentiles" (τὸ εὐαγγέλιον ὃ κηρύσσω ἐν τοῖς ἔθνεσιν) links back to "proclaim him among the gentiles" (εὐαγγελίζωμαι αὐτὸν ἐν τοῖς ἔθνεσιν) in 1:16 (and also to 1:6, 7, 8 [2x], 9, 11, 23).

82. Some think that "them" refers to the Christians in Jerusalem and involves a public meeting, and that a separate private meeting happened with the Jerusalem apostles. I see only one meeting, with Paul clarifying whom he means by "them" as "those who appear to be important." See Moo, *Galatians*, s.vv. "Second Jerusalem Visit: The 'Pillars' Confirm Paul's Gospel" (Gal 2:1–10).

83. Paul's portrayed these apostles as the community perceives them rather than who they inherently are (Moo, *Galatians*, s.vv. "Second Jerusalem Visit: The Pillars' Confirm Paul's Gospel" [Gal 2:1–10]).

84. While there is much uncertainty and disagreement about whether Paul is describing the same council that Luke recounts in Acts 15 or a meeting that took place during the famine relief trip to Jerusalem (Acts 11:27–30), the emphasis on the private nature in 2:2 leads me to favor the latter. Moreover, it seems unlikely that Paul would risk being accused of omitting an important visit to Jerusalem. If Gal 2:1–10 corresponds to Acts 15, then Paul would have skipped over the famine relief visit. See especially Moo, *Galatians*, s.vv. "Chronological Considerations"; Schnabel, *Paul and the Early Church*, 989–91.

his gospel's truth, their agreement was vital from a practical perspective.[85] The destructive influence Cephas had when he acted contrary to the gospel in Antioch provides a prime example of what could happen (which explains why Paul had to confront and correct him in 2:11–21).

With Paul finally presenting the gospel he proclaimed among the gentiles after nearly two decades operating independently of the apostles in Jerusalem, one might expect that they might correct or add something (Paul would go on to expressly deny that they added anything in 2:6). Given the Galatian believers' apparent receptive acceptance of the premise that gentile Christians need to follow Jewish customs (epitomized by the rite of circumcision), they might have expected the apostles in Jerusalem to endorse the need to circumcise gentile Christians. Titus (who had accompanied Paul to Jerusalem) was before the Jerusalem apostles in person. Surely, they would insist that Titus be circumcised. Contrary to the Galatians' expectations (ἀλλά),[86] however, not even Titus, who was with Paul, who is Greek,[87] was compelled to be circumcised (2:3).[88] Here, Paul partially spoils the story's happy ending before circling back to describe how things got there.

Paul attaches substantial symbolic implications to the decision not to compel Titus to be circumcised. It signifies that the Jerusalem apostles supported Paul's law-free gospel for gentiles. While this is the first time the practice of circumcision is mentioned in the letter,[89] Paul's choice of the

---

85. Schreiner, *Galatians*, 122.

86. On the discourse function of ἀλλά to replace an incorrect expectation with a proper one, see Runge, *Discourse Grammar*, 93.

87. See Moo on how Paul uses "Greek" ("Ελλην), just like ἔθνη, to refer to gentiles or non-Jews (*Galatians*, s.vv. "Second Jerusalem Visit: The 'Pillars' Confirm Paul's Gospel" [Gal 2:1–10]). Schreiner helpfully explains how the case of Timothy (who was considered a Jew due to his mother being Jewish) differed from Titus (*Galatians*, 124).

88. Moo explains οὐδὲ Τίτος ὁ σὺν ἐμοί similarly (*Galatians*, s.vv. "Second Jerusalem Visit: The 'Pillars' Confirm Paul's Gospel" [Gal 2:1–10]). I would add that the ἀλλά fits within this same explanation. It is not necessary to take it with the negative purpose clause at the end of v. 2, as Moo does in saying that "Paul feared that his ministry among the Gentiles might have been in vain, but, in fact, his law-free gospel for the Gentiles was vindicated, as evidenced in the critical decision not to compel Titus to be circumcised." In this alternative interpretation, it would be Paul's dim expectation of the Jerusalem apostles that was corrected.

89. See also 2:7, 8, 9, 12; 5:2, 3, 6, 11; 6:12, 13, 15. In the Old Testament, circumcision served as a mark of inclusion in God's covenant people. Those who refused circumcision were considered outside of God's covenant (Gen 17:9–14). During Paul's era, Second Temple Judaism debated whether circumcision remained obligatory for gentile converts to Judaism. While some opinions differed, the majority upheld the Old Testament's teachings and mandated circumcision for inclusion in God's covenant people. As seen from Acts 15:1, 5, some Jews who believed in Jesus as the Messiah also maintained that gentiles must undergo circumcision and adhere to the law of Moses for salvation (Schreiner, *Galatians*, 123).

verb "compel" (ἠναγκάσθη) closely ties the decision on circumcision to the broader issue he was addressing in Galatia. The cause of contention is more fully expressed in the other two places where this verb appears:

1. "When I saw that they were not acting in line with the truth of the gospel, I said to Cephas in front of them all, 'You are a Jew, yet you live like a gentile and not like a Jew. How is it, then, that you force [ἀναγκάζεις] gentiles to follow Jewish customs?'" (2:14)

2. "Those who want to impress others by means of the flesh are trying to compel [ἀναγκάζουσιν] you to be circumcised. Their only purpose [μόνον ἵνα] is to avoid being persecuted for the cross of Christ." (6:12)[90]

Paul adds a new point (δὲ) to correct the Galatians' expectations and perceptions in v. 4: they have these false perceptions "because of false brothers." Like how he undermined the other gospel his opponents proclaimed (1:6–7) and pronounced them cursed (1:8–9), Paul undermines the credibility of similar opponents in this past episode. He paints them as "false brothers" (ψευδαδέλφους) who had sneaked in (παρεισάκτους). He does not stop there, further describing them as "who had slipped in to spy out our freedom that we have in Christ Jesus, in order to enslave us" (οἵτινες παρεισῆλθον κατασκοπῆσαι τὴν ἐλευθερίαν ἡμῶν ἣν ἔχομεν ἐν Χριστῷ Ἰησοῦ, ἵνα ἡμᾶς καταδουλώσουσιν). This foreshadows the contrast between freedom in Christ Jesus and slavery later in the letter (e.g., 4:21–31; 5:1, 13).[91] Whether the opponents in Jerusalem and the opponents in Galatia belong to the same group in a formal sense or not, Paul effectively associates them together. He brands their so-called gospel as resulting in slavery rather than the freedom of the true gospel.[92]

---

90. Moo, *Galatians*, s.vv. "Second Jerusalem Visit: The 'Pillars' Confirm Paul's Gospel" (Gal 2:1–10).

91. DeSilva, *Galatians*, 178; Schreiner, *Galatians*, 125.

92. As Moo notes, given that most Jews in Paul's era believed that gentile coverts to Judaism had to be circumcised for inclusion in God's covenant people, the issue of circumcision is sure to arise wherever gentiles "began associating with Jews within a single 'Messianic' community" (*Galatians*, s.vv. "Second Jerusalem Visit: The 'Pillars' Confirm Paul's Gospel" [Gal 2:1–10]). It is not surprising to see similar views advocated by these false brothers in Jerusalem, the agitators in Galatia, the people from Judea who were teaching in Antioch (Acts 15:1), and some from the party of the Pharisees at the Jerusalem Council (15:5).

After building a thoroughly negative portrait of his opponents in v. 4, Paul reveals in v. 5 his and his companions'[93] resolute opposition to them[94] and the purpose or stakes involved for the Galatians: "to whom not even for a moment[95] did we yield in submission in order that the truth of the gospel might remain with you."[96]

Even "those who appear to be important" in v. 2 are taken down a notch. Whether or not referring to them as "those who seem to be something" in itself casts doubt on their importance, Paul makes this point clear. Whatever they were made no difference to him as they added nothing to him. Indeed, God's viewpoint is even plainer: God pays no attention to human stature (2:6).[97]

In v. 9, the happy ending is spelled out. Contrary to the adding or correction of things that others might have expected (ἀλλὰ τοὐναντίον), those thought to be pillars (explicitly named as James, Cephas [i.e., Peter], and John) extended the right hand of fellowship to Paul and Barnabas, effectively affirming Paul's gospel and calling.

Paul carefully sets the scene between vv. 7 and 9 before getting to this central point.[98] James, Peter, and John affirmed Paul's gospel and calling because they saw and knew something. First, they saw that Paul had been entrusted with the gospel for the uncircumcised, just as Peter had been for the circumcised (2:7).[99] Verse 8 supports (γὰρ) Paul's claim that God had entrusted Paul and Peter with comparable but different ministries. This is because the one who worked in Peter for apostleship for the circumcised also worked in Paul for the gentiles. In v. 9, Paul adds (καὶ) the second

---

93. As Runge notes, based on the preceding discourse, the Galatian believers would naturally assume that "we" refers only to Paul, Barnabas, and Titus (*Galatians*, Gal 2:1–10).

94. Paul's response of not yielding in submission to them even for a moment (οἷς οὐδὲ πρὸς ὥραν εἴξαμεν τῇ ὑποταγῇ) opposes and frustrates their desire to enslave Paul and other believers (ἵνα ἡμᾶς καταδουλώσουσιν). There is a poorly attested textual variant that changes the sense to Paul actually submitting for a short while, but there is no reason to think it is original. See Bruce, *Galatians*, 113–15.

95. As Moo notes, "An 'hour' was the shortest demarcation of time in Paul's day, so the phrase οὐδὲ πρὸς ὥραν means 'not even for a moment'" (*Galatians*, s.vv. "Second Jerusalem Visit: The 'Pillars' Confirm Paul's Gospel" [Gal 2:1–10]).

96. The Galatian believers would naturally understand "you" to refer to themselves and possibly by extension other gentile believers (Longenecker, *Galatians*, 53).

97. Schreiner, *Galatians*, 126–28.

98. Runge, *Galatians*, Gal 2:1–10.

99. Yoon notes that πεπίστευμαι is the only perfect tense form (stative aspect) in 1:11—2:10 ("Prominence in New Testament," 22). While I agree that it is prominent in the local context, it is inside a content clause. So, it is prominent only in the offline perception event in 2:7–9 and not in the mainline event of 2:1–10.

reason he received affirmation: James, Peter, and John recognized the grace given to Paul.

The scene-setting statements in vv. 7–9 make clear that the pillars of the Jerusalem church saw and recognized the divine origin of Paul's message and calling and affirmed them.[100] This affirmation came in the form of extending the right hand of fellowship to Paul and Barnabas. The purpose was so that Paul and Barnabas might continue to minister to the gentiles and the pillars to the circumcised (i.e., the Jews).

It is only after making all the above abundantly clear that Paul mentions that the Jerusalem leaders did make one request, namely to remember the poor (i.e., the poorer members of the Jerusalem church, as in Rom 15:26). However, this was something he was already eager to do (2:10). It was, in fact, his established practice. Acts 11:27–30, for example, shows Paul's track record of helping the poor.[101] By mentioning this request only to deny that it was something new, Paul reinforces his point that the Jerusalem leaders did not add a single thing to his message or practice.[102]

E. Confronted and Corrected Cephas When He Obscured Truth of the Gospel (2:11–21)

Table 17: The Flow of 2:11–21

Connector	At	Connects	With	Function
Ὅτε δὲ	2:11	2:11–21	1:12—2:10	Next (distinct point)
γὰρ	2:12a	2:12–13	2:11	Supports
ὅτε δὲ	2:12b	2:12b–13	2:12a	Contrast (after and before)
καὶ	2:13a	2:13a	2:12b	Associated (response)
ὥστε	2:13b	2:13b	2:12b–13a	Result
ἀλλ'	2:14	2:14–21	2:11–13	Corrects (in contrast)
Inclusive "we" and closely related concept	2:15	2:15	2:14	Describes (common knowledge)
δὲ	2:16	2:16	2:15	Elaborates (common knowledge)

---

100. DeSilva, *Galatians*, 181–82.
101. Schreiner, *Galatians*, 131.
102. Runge, *Galatians*, Gal 2:1–10.

δέ	2:17	2:17	2:15–16	Elaborates (potential objection)
γάρ	2:18	2:18–20	2:17	Supports (denial of objection)
γάρ	2:19a	2:19–20	2:18	Supports
Closely related concept	2:19b	2:19b	2:19a	Elaborates (by restatement)
δέ (3x)	2:20	2:20	2:19b	Elaborates
Closely related concept	2:21a	2:21a	2:14–20	Response (in light of 2:14–20)
γάρ	2:21b	2:21b	2:21a	Supports

In 2:11–21, we come to the culminating piece of evidence that Paul's gospel had a divine rather than human origin, which is the main point supported by the whole of 1:13—2:21.[103] Paul describes an astounding scene: when no less a leading figure as Cephas erred and stood condemned in relation to the gospel message, Paul confronted and corrected him to his face (2:11). This is the main point Paul draws from this incident. The Greek word order highlights both the manner and reason behind the confrontation. Paul cleverly positions this story as the climax of his argument. The principles applied in Antioch mirror those needed in the Galatian churches. It is a story about Peter in Antioch. It also clearly applies to the Galatian churches. Nevertheless, as will become evident in the following discussion, I see the entirety of 2:11–21 as primarily addressed to Cephas.[104]

What did Cephas do to merit this rebuke? Paul now circles back to explain what happened. Paul identifies the arrival of certain individuals from James as a turning point, which sets up a before-and-after comparison (2:12). He presents it as the sole explanation for a significant shift in fellowship practices. Among Cephas's activities, Paul focuses solely on his table fellowship with gentiles. This act, whether specific to communion or shared meals in general, defies Jewish tradition, which deems mingling with gentiles ritually impure. Before these individuals from James came, Cephas used to eat together with the gentiles. After they arrived,[105] Cephas stopped

---

103. Runge shares this conclusion, though with some notable differences (*Galatians*, Gal 2:11–14).

104. While differing on some points, Schreiner likewise sees all of 2:14–21 as addressed to Cephas (*Galatians*, 150). See also Keener, *Galatians*, s.vv. "Made Right with God Through Christ Alone" (Gal 2:15–21); Parunak, "Dimensions of Discourse Structure," 236.

105. Some normally reliable early witnesses have a singular (rather than plural)

doing so. In fact, rather than simply stating that Peter stopped eating with gentiles, Paul portrays his actions as withdrawal and separation. The term "withdraw" suggests a retreat out of fear, as seen in Acts 20, where Paul emphasizes not shrinking from preaching the gospel. The second action, "separation," can involve a positive selection or a negative removal, depending on the context. Paul deliberately frames Cephas's response in a negative light. Any ambiguity is removed by attributing Cephas's actions to "fear of the circumcision."[106]

Notably, Paul did not simply say that Cephas and the other Jewish Christians stopped eating with gentiles. Instead, he singled out Cephas first. Then, he noted that the remaining Jewish believers joined Cephas in hypocrisy. Indeed, the tide of negative influence was so strong as to result in even (ὥστε καὶ) Barnabas (Paul's fellow leader in the mission to the gentiles) being led astray by their hypocrisy (2:13).[107]

Given such powerful peer pressure, what did Paul do? In contrast to everyone else who bowed to peer pressure (ἀλλ'), when Paul saw his fellow Jewish Christians' actions, he rebuked Cephas publicly before everyone. Indeed, he offers his assessment of what was really happening: They were not walking straight in regard to the truth of the gospel (2:14). Given Paul's history of standing up for the truth of the gospel (2:5), we are not surprised by his response when he sees another occasion where the truth of the gospel is at stake.[108]

Paul begins with a rhetorical question that makes it difficult to disagree with his argument: if Cephas, despite being a Jew, really lived like a gentile and not like a Jew, then what Paul argues naturally follows (2:14). We know Paul's thesis that Cephas lived like a gentile is true because Cephas had been eating with the gentiles before certain individuals came from James (v. 12).[109] The interrogative then asks a question that expects a negative answer. Of course, Cephas cannot do that. In a context where Cephas and the Jewish Christians

---

verb. One early witness has the singular "someone." The first may be an error from assimilating to surrounding singular verbs and might have led to the second error. See Moo, *Galatians*, s.vv. "An Incident at Antioch: Paul Defends the Gospel" (Gal 2:11–14), "Additional Notes."

106. Runge, *Galatians*, Gal 2:11–14.

107. Runge, *Galatians*, Gal 2:11–14.

108. In a private email, Mark Seifrid indicated that he is inclined to read 2:1–21 as a single (two-part) unit. As evident from table 12, "Overview of the Flow of 1:13—2:21," I see the five parts of 1:13–17, 18–20, 21–24; 2:1–10, 11–21 as parallel, with the γὰρ in 1:13 signaling all five parts as acting in support. Nevertheless, I agree with Mark that reading 2:11–21 right after 2:1–10 effectively "underscores Paul's steadfastness and Cephas' failure" (Seifrid, email, ca. Aug. 2024).

109. Nicolle, "Conditionals in Galatians," 96.

have already been characterized as acting hypocritically by not behaving consistently with the truth of the gospel, this rhetorical question serves as a powerful rebuke.[110] It draws Cephas to agree with Paul's implied negative evaluation.[111] This is the main point of Paul's speech, which elaborates on the error for which he confronted Cephas. Besides identifying "the truth of the gospel" as implicated in both situations, the word "compel" (ἀναγκάζεις) elicits a comparison of Cephas with the false brothers in 2:3–5. Cephas was practically compelling the gentile Christians to become Jews, just like the false brothers tried to "compel" (ἠναγκάσθη [2:3]) Titus to be circumcised.[112] This was inconsistent with what Cephas really believed and should not be.

Paul continues his argument by including himself with Cephas and other Jewish Christians using "we." They share a common ground in being born Jews (Jews by nature) and not sinners from the gentiles (2:15).[113] In my view, a standard Jewish view of gentiles as sinners because they do not keep Jewish traditions is in view here.

In addition (δὲ),[114] they share a common knowledge and also a common faith in Christ (2:16). While there is significant controversy about whether to read ἐὰν μὴ as except, I believe Paul states that what Jewish Christians like himself know is this: No one is justified by works associated with the law except through faith associated with Christ.[115] It is essential to realize that Jewish Christians, except for those like Cephas and others who were involved in the mission to the gentiles, generally continued to keep Jewish traditions. Continuing to keep Jewish traditions (as most Jewish Christians did) did not inherently disqualify one from being justified. Otherwise, all those Jewish Christians would have been in trouble. The only problem was to insist that the works of the law either contributed towards or were necessary to be justified before God. This renders doing what the

---

110. Similarly, Verster, "Nonauthentic Questions in Galatians," 150–51.

111. This type of rhetorical question states an evaluation, expressing approval or disapproval. In cases of disapproval, it reflects negatively on the legitimacy of one's purpose, reason, or motive. See Beekman and Callow, *Translating Word of God*, 243–44.

112. Schreiner, *Galatians*, 147–48. Schreiner also helpfully points out that unlike the false brothers, Cephas and the Jewish believers have already proven in their prior actions that they do not actually believe that you have to live like a Jew to be part of God's people. So, Paul rebukes and corrects them, but does not identify them as false brothers.

113. Similarly, Yoon points out that Paul and Peter are the "we" who are Jews by nature and that the "we" connects 2:15 to 2:11–14 ("End of Paul's Speech," 77–78).

114. This marker is omitted in a significant part of the manuscript tradition. With or without this explicit marker, I would read v. 16 as closely connected to v. 15 and as adding a point that develops things further.

115. Similarly, Runge, *Galatians*, Gal 2:14b–21.

law requires totally irrelevant as far as justification is concerned. Jews who continued to observe Jewish traditions believed in Christ Jesus precisely because faith in Jesus Christ is the only way to be justified before God.[116]

Indeed, Paul spells this understanding out clearly when he expresses the purpose that Jews like him have believed in Christ Jesus. Because no one[117] can be justified by the works of the law, even Jewish Christians must be justified through faith in Christ and not through the works of the law (2:16).

Paul proceeds (δὲ) by cutting off a potential objection. If Jewish Christians are also themselves found to be sinners while seeking to be justified in Christ, does that make Christ a servant of sin? "Also ourselves sinners" (καὶ αὐτοὶ ἁμαρτωλοί) connects back to "sinners from the gentiles" (ἐξ ἐθνῶν ἁμαρτωλοί) in 2:15.[118] In my view, the same standard Jewish perception of gentiles as sinners because they do not keep Jewish traditions is carried over here. So, if Jewish Christians like Paul, Cephas, and others who are involved in the mission to the gentiles are found to be sinners like the gentiles precisely because they no longer keep the works of the law, does that then (ἄρα) make Christ a servant of sin? Paul emphatically denies this conclusion (2:17).

At first glance, it is not apparent how the next argument bolsters Paul's point that Christ does not promote sin. However, it helps to recall that Jewish Christians would also be found to be sinners like gentiles when they stopped keeping Jewish law. Paul is appealing to the common situation where he, Cephas, and the other Jewish believers involved in the gentile mission had already stopped living like Jews. They know that no one is justified by the works of the law. They previously ate with the gentiles, living out their conviction that the law was irrelevant to being justified before God. So, they know that seeking to be justified in Christ does not promote sin. Paul

---

116. The genitive constructions "the works associated with the law" and "the faith associated with Christ" do not in themselves specify the exact relationship between works and the law or faith and Christ. The works, in some sense, have to do with the law. Likewise, the faith, in some sense, has to do with Christ. See Porter and Pitts, "Πίστις," 38–48. Because I am applying the principle of interpreting Galatians with Galatians first and foremost, the explicit spelling out of "we have believed in Christ" in a verbal clause in 2:16 is enough reason to tentatively interpret "the faith associated with Christ" as "faith in Christ." The meanings of the words "works" and "law" in themselves lead me tentatively to "doing what the law requires" as laws inherently tell you what to do. Like Keener (*Galatians*, s.vv. "A Closer Look: 'Christ-Faith'" [Gal 2:16; 3:22]), I believe that the text of Galatians is more intelligible when read this way. So, I will mostly wait to point out the relevant evidence as we continue to read through the text.

117. "All flesh" (πᾶσα σάρξ) merely means all humanity here.

118. Nicolle, "Conditionals in Galatians," 97–98.

applies a situation to himself hypothetically that actually applied to Cephas and the other Jewish Christians who followed Cephas in hypocrisy.[119] The Jewish law is the building he describes himself hypothetically rebuilding or tearing down metaphorically. This is actually not true of Paul. Previously, Cephas and the others were also united with Paul in affirming and living out the fact that both Jewish Christians who stopped keeping Jewish law and gentile Christians who do not keep that law are not sinners in God's eyes. However, their recent hypocrisy shows them to be transgressors of the law by abandoning it only to return to it (2:18). This recalls Paul's characterization of Cephas as condemned in v. 11.

After challenging Cephas and the Jewish Christian with him to consider the implications of their hypocritical return to law keeping, Paul continues in the first person. He is sharing his own experience as support. However, this should also be the experience of Cephas and the other Jewish Christians. Paul is drawing his wayward brothers to identify their own experiences with his experience to help bring them back to the right path. Paul engages in further explanations (γὰρ) that would be somewhat cryptic to those who do not share his understanding of the Scriptures. What does he mean by "for through the law I died to the law so that I might live to God" (2:19)? It appears that he is encapsulating his understanding of the law and the Christian life in very concise form here before circling back to spell things out further in the rest of 2:19–21 as well as in more detail later in the letter.[120] For now, it is enough to observe that, in some sense, by passing through the law, Paul died to the law so that he might live for God.[121] In addition, Paul clarifies that his death to the law through the law has something to do with being crucified together with Christ (2:19).[122] Moreover, in some sense, Paul no longer lives (2:20).

119. Nicolle, "Conditionals in Galatians," 98–99.

120. Longenecker, *Galatians*, 91. Moo points out the key words first introduced in 2:15–21 that are taken up later in the letter: νόμος (law, 6x here, 27x later); ἔργα νόμου (works of the law, 3x here, 3x later); δικαιόω (justify, 4x here, 4x later); δικαιοσύνη (righteousness, 1x here, 3x later); πίστις (faith, 3x here, 18x later); πιστεύω (believe, 1x here, 2x later); and ζάω (live, 5x here, 3x later). (πίστις and πιστεύω do occur once each before 2:15–21, but in a different sense) (*Galatians*, s.vv. "The Truth of the Gospel Defined" [Gal 2:15–21]). While Paul uses more than key words to develop his themes, these key words are helpful in tracing the connections of 2:15–21 to later parts of the letter.

121. The contrast between θεῷ and νόμῳ is focal and central to Paul's argument (Levinsohn, *Discourse Features* 9.3).

122. Paul elaborates on "through the law I died to the law so that I might live to God" with four further points in 2:19–21: (1) I have been crucified with Christ; (2) I no longer live; (3) Christ lives in me; and (4) the life I now live in the body I live by faith in the Son of God, who loved me and gave himself for me. Similarly, Levinsohn, "Galatians," 314.

What about Paul living for God? Verse 20 further reveals that it involves Christ in some sense living in Paul. Verse 21 shows that this, in turn, involves living the life he lives in his body by faith in Christ. So, Paul has been crucified together with Christ and has died. However, he also still lives in his body by faith in Christ. In so doing, Christ also lives in him. It is noteworthy that Paul characterizes Christ as "the son of God who loved me and gave himself for me."[123] Paul reinforces his emphasis on Christ's giving of himself ("gave himself for our sins" [1:3]) in how he wants his readers to relate to Christ.

Unlike Cephas and the Jewish Christians with him, Paul does not reject the grace of God.[124] However, they would agree with Paul that Christ did not die for nothing. Therefore, they also agree that righteousness could not come through the law.[125] Hypothetically, if righteousness could come through the law (which Cephas and the Jewish Christians' behavior imply), then (ἄρα) Christ really did die for nothing (2:21).[126] This shows that their behavior is inconsistent with their beliefs and tantamount to rejecting God's grace. When reading this strong statement from Paul, the Galatians would also recall Paul's conceptually related rebuke of them for turning away from the one who called them in the grace of Christ (1:6). The Galatians' behavior likewise carries the same implications. So, they should recognize that, like Cephas, they too stood condemned and needed to change course.

---

123. Some early witnesses read "God and Christ" rather than "the Son of God." This reading might refer to the faithfulness of God and Christ, given that Paul does not speak elsewhere of God as the object of faith. See Moo, *Galatians*, s.vv. "The Truth of the Gospel Defined" (Gal 2:15–21), "Additional Notes."

124. This statement would undoubtedly call to mind Paul's conceptually related rebuke of the Galatians for turning away from the one who called you in the grace of Christ (1:6).

125. As Moo notes, Paul's argument from 2:21 to 3:21 goes like this: Since Christ did not die in vain, righteousness does not come through the law (2:21). Then, since righteousness does not come through the law, no law that is able to make alive has been given (3:21) (*Galatians*, s.vv. "The Law in Salvation History" [Gal 3:15–25]).

126. Nicolle, "Conditionals in Galatians," 99.

GALATIANS 3:1—4:7

OUTLINE

II. First Round of Rebuke, Backed by Extended Support (1:6—2:21)

III. Second Round of Rebuke, Backed by Extended Support (3:1—4:7)
    A. Double-Layered Rebuke (3:1–6)
    B. Only Those Who Rely on Faith Are Abraham's True Heirs (3:7—4:7)

III. SECOND ROUND OF REBUKE, BACKED BY EXTENDED SUPPORT (3:1—4:7)

Paul begins a second round of rebuke after supporting his self-portrayal as a servant of Christ and proclaiming a divine rather than human gospel at length (1:10—2:21). He finally returns to addressing the churches of Galatia directly and challenges them with six rhetorical questions in 3:1–5.[1] If you already have a shared understanding of Paul's calling and gospel, you can read ch. 3 directly after 1:6–9 without missing much. Paul defends his calling and message precisely because they were in dispute in the original situational context of the letter. Now that we know that 1:10—2:21 is all supporting material, we can see that the first main point was: I am astonished that you are so quickly turning away from the divine gospel brought to you by a divinely appointed servant of Christ. We expect to find the second main

---

1. Runge comes to a similar assessment (*Galatians*, Gal 3:1–18). The change in participants and speech functions as well as the lack of a conjunction together signal a new section at 3:1 (Yoon, "End of Paul's Speech," 71–78). Levinsohn likewise identifies 3:1 as the major division and includes these factors as well as a few other weaker indicators ("Discourse Analysis: Galatians," 118–19).

point in the next rebuke-focused paragraph. For reasons we will see later, I identify the second main point as: O foolish Galatians, I want to learn from you whether you received the Spirit through doing what the law requires or through hearing accompanied by faith.

In this chapter, we will dive into the details of each section within 3:1—4:7. Table 18 below provides an overview of the discourse flow for 3:1—4:7 as a whole.

Table 18: Overview of the Flow of 3:1—4:7				
Connector	At	Connects	With	Function
None	3:1			Major break (starts second-round rebuke)
Closely related concepts	3:2–5	3:2–5	3:1	Related questions that challenge Galatians' foolishness on the basis of their own experiences
Καθώς	3:6	3:6	3:1–5	Compares (Abraham's experience with Galatians' experience)
ἄρα	3:7	3:7–14	3:6	Infers (from 3:6 that only those who rely on faith are Abraham's children)
None	3:15	3:15–18	3:7–14	Minor break (permanence of God's promise)
οὖν	3:19a	3:19–22	3:15–18	Infers (question on the law's role)
Closely related concepts	3:19b	3:19b–22	3:19a	Answers (question on the law's role)
δέ	3:23	3:23–29	3:15–22	Elaborates (on situation before faith and after faith)
δέ	4:1	4:1–7	3:15–29	Elaborates (on status of the promise's heirs)

Galatians 3:1–6 is the start of a second round of rebuke. How does Paul rebuke the Galatians? Whereas in 1:6—2:21 Paul's rebuke focuses on how inconceivable it is based on the divine origin of both his apostleship and message, in 3:1—4:7, Paul's rebuke focuses on why their actions are foolish. Galatians 3:1–5 in this rebuke-focused paragraph asks a series of rhetorical questions that challenge the Galatians' foolishness based on their own experiences of receiving the Spirit through faith rather than through doing what the law requires. It is precisely because of this fact that their actions are so mind boggling. Their experience should have kept them on

their original path. In fact, their experience compares well with Abraham's experience (3:6), which leads to the conclusion that only those who rely on faith are Abraham's true children (3:7–14). The fact that God graciously gave the inheritance to Abraham through a promise guarantees the enduring validity of God's promise (3:15–18). While this raises questions about the law's role, there is a good answer: it was meant to shut in all under sin, so that the promise might be given by means of faith in Jesus Christ to those who believe (3:19–22). The law had a role before faith came into play, but it ended after faith arrived on the scene (3:23–29). The children of God whom Christ redeemed are heirs who have come of age and come into their inheritance (4:1–7).

A. Double-Layered Rebuke (3:1–6)

Table 19: The Flow of 3:1–6				
Connector	At	Connects	With	Function
None	3:1			Major break (starts second-round rebuke)
Closely related concepts	3:2	3:2–5	3:1	Challenges (based on past experience)
Closely related concepts	3:3	3:3	3:1–2	Reinforces (challenge by restatement)
Demonstrative	3:4	3:4	3:1–3	Reinforces (challenge by referring to 3:1–3)
οὖν	3:5	3:5	3:2–4	Infers (from 3:2–4 to reinforce challenge)
Καθώς	3:6	3:6	3:2–5	Compares (with Abraham's experience)

While the Galatian Christians were probably aware that Paul disagreed with them, they were almost certainly shocked to learn that Paul viewed them as foolish. Paul not only gets their attention with a direct address but also paints them in a very negative light. Indeed, he will challenge them again about being foolish in v. 3.[2]

By highlighting his evaluation of the Galatians as foolish, Paul also indicates that his rhetorical question is meant as a rebuke. Moreover, despite this first rhetorical question, he is not interested in the identity of the

2. Runge, *Galatians*, Gal 3:1–18.

perpetrators. How do we know this? First, he quickly moves away to other questions without answering who these perpetrators were. Second, Paul has previously dismissed them as "those who are confusing you and who want to distort the gospel of Christ" (1:7). Moreover, he has cursed anyone who proclaims a gospel other than what the Galatian churches have previously received (1:8–9). If no one could legitimately lead the Galatians to follow a different gospel, then the fact that someone has bewitched them to do that cannot and should not happen. Instead of seeking an answer about the identity of his opponents, Paul's point is: How can it be that someone has seemingly bewitched them (as with a spell) to the point that they do not perceive the significance of Christ crucified?[3]

Paul sharpens his portrait of foolishness by describing the Galatian Christians he had in mind: they are those to whom the crucified Christ has been proclaimed right before their eyes (3:1). Even though this is the start of a new section, this accusation about failure to perceive the significance of Christ crucified comes immediately after 2:21, where their behavior that implies righteousness could come through the law is depicted as rendering Christ's death meaningless. So, through his story about Cephas's failure, Paul has already indirectly indicted the Galatians for the very thing with which he now directly charges them. In addition, Paul will elaborate further in 3:7—4:7 (especially 3:7-14; 4:4-7) why the Galatians are foolish for not realizing the significance of Christ crucified.

For now, Paul focuses on the second layer of his rebuke. He wants the Galatian Christians to recognize that they had received the Spirit through "hearing associated with faith" rather than "works associated with the law." In 2:16, we previously noted how genitive constructions do not in themselves specify the exact relationship between the two nouns in the construction. When the genitive phrases need to be mentioned multiple times, it will be unwieldy to keep saying "associated with." So, I will often use "of" for convenience's sake. However, I mean "of" in the sense of "associated with" with such genitive constructions. With a contrast between works and hearing, a contrast between the acts of doing and hearing naturally suggests themselves first and foremost. So, by "works of the law" and "hearing of faith," my tentative interpretation of the opposition involves doing what the law requires versus hearing accompanied by faith.[4]

---

3. There is a textual variant that adds "to not obey the truth" (τῇ ἀληθείᾳ μὴ πείθεσθαι) after "bewitched you." The manuscript evidence is not strong. As Bruce notes, the same words do occur in 5:7, and that passage likely influenced the addition of these words here (*Galatians*, 147–48).

4. Similarly, Moo, *Galatians*, s.vv. "Rebuke and Reminder: Faith, Spirit, and Righteousness" (Gal 3:1–6). This interpretation of how hearing is associated with faith is also

Instead of asserting directly that his audience had received the Spirit through "hearing of faith,"[5] Paul challenges them with another rhetorical question that makes the choice between "hearing of faith" and "works of the law" clear. He also draws further attention to this question by using a forward-pointing reference: this only I wish to learn from you.[6] Galatians 3:2 is also reinforced by the similar rhetorical question inferred in 3:5. So, 3:2 is the main point of 3:1–6 and 3:1—4:7 as a whole.[7] When the Galatians reflect on their own experience, they would come to the obvious conclusion that "hearing of faith" is the answer. Paul adds a third rebuking rhetorical question: Are you so foolish? This reinforces Paul's portrayal of the Galatians as foolish in 3:1. The fourth rhetorical question pinpoints the nature of the foolishness: After beginning in the Spirit, are you now trying to finish in the flesh? (3:3).[8] Paul characterizes receiving the Spirit through the hearing of faith as beginning with the Spirit. By contrast, works of the law are associated with trying to finish the journey (which they started in the Spirit) in the flesh.[9]

Paul further reinforces his rebuke by rhetorically asking if the Galatian churches have experienced so much in vain. While it is possible that the demonstrative τοσαῦτα refers to commonly known sufferings not mentioned in the text, it seems better to see the demonstrative as referring to the previous statements. So, Paul would be pointing to their experience of having the crucified Christ proclaimed right before their eyes and having received the Spirit through hearing of faith.[10] By adding "if indeed it really is in vain"

---

consistent with Paul's portrayal in Rom 10:17. ἀκοή refers to the message proclaimed in Rom 10:16, but the act of hearing in 10:17 (Schreiner, *Galatians*, 183).

5. As Levinsohn notes, the most important information in this given setting is how the Galatians received the Spirit (*Discourse Features* 2.1).

6. The whole extra statement announcing what Paul wants to know (instead of simply asking the question) serves as a forward-pointing reference to draw attention to the question that follows (Runge, *Galatians*, Gal 3:1–18). See Levinsohn, "Galatians," 316–17.

7. It is also the main support for rebuking them as foolish. That's why I included the characterization as foolish in how I stated the main point in my heading for this section.

8. "Beginning in the Spirit" recalls "received the Spirit" in 3:2.

9. Paired with the middle ἐναρξάμενοι (having begun), ἐπιτελεῖσθε likely is also middle, in the sense of "finish" or "bring to completion." See Moo, *Galatians*, s.vv. "Rebuke and Reminder: Faith, Spirit, and Righteousness" (Gal 3:1–6). "Flesh" likely evokes circumcision, which is carried out in the body. However, set in contrast with the Spirit (received through faith), flesh here takes on the nuance of merely human means available outside of faith. Similarly, Bruce, *Galatians*, 149.

10. While suffering cannot be ruled out as part of their experiences, in this context, Paul has explicitly mentioned their experiences of the proclamation of the crucified and reception of the Spirit through faith. Explicit experiences should be favored over experiences that are not mentioned in the text. Similarly, see DeSilva, *Galatians*, 275–76.

(3:4), Paul expresses his doubt of a negative outcome and leaves the door open for them to change course.[11]

After getting the Galatians to evaluate their own experiences, Paul challenges them with a sixth rhetorical question in v. 5. He wants them to recognize an objective fact about God: Based on their own experience of God's prior work among them (οὖν),[12] does the one who supplies you with the Spirit and works miracles among you do it by works of law or by hearing with faith? In v. 2, their hearts would have resonated with the implied answer that they had received the Spirit through hearing with faith. Here, too, their hearts would have affirmed that it was by hearing with faith that God had supplied them with the Spirit and worked miracles among them.[13] Indeed, the contrast between faith and works of the law ties together the experiences of Jewish Christians and gentile Christians alike. The Galatians themselves are witnesses through their personal experiences. Their experiences would confirm Paul's negative assessment against them. In addition, Paul compares their experience with Abraham's experience of being counted righteous through faith (3:6).[14] Crucially, in making the comparison, Paul uses the verb "believe," which confirms that the noun "faith" in the contrast between "hearing of faith" and "works of the law" has to do with "believing." Abraham himself (the ancestor of the Jewish people) serves as a historical precedent on the path of faith.[15]

B. Only Those Who Rely on Faith Are Abraham's True Heirs (3:7—4:7)

After directly challenging the Galatians with six rhetorical questions in 3:1–5, Paul does not resume his direct rebuke until 4:8–9. Instead, he musters a series of arguments from Scripture to support his rebuke before he resumes

---

11. Nicolle, "Conditionals in Galatians," 100.

12. οὖν draws a conclusion from 3:2–4, effectively making 3:2–4 the support for 3:5.

13. As Runge notes, this rhetorical question acts "as a hinge, summarizing the conclusion drawn from verses 1–4 and introducing what becomes the key idea through verse 14. The question is the same he has posed to the Galatians in [3]:2–3, but now he considers the other side of the equation. What ultimately moves God to act, faith or works?" (*Galatians*, Gal 3:1–18). Levinsohn observes that "the implied answer to the rhetorical question of 3:5 (it is by believing what you heard that God supplies you with the Spirit and works miracles among you), together with the conclusion of 3:14b (. . . 'so that we might receive the promise of the Spirit through faith') . . . is the 'linchpin of Paul's argument'" ("Galatians," 316).

14. Silva, *Interpreting Galatians*, 253.

15. DeSilva, *Galatians*, 277.

doing so. The comparison to Abraham's experience in v. 6 sets Paul up to argue from Scripture in this next long section. The main point in 3:7–14 and 3:7—4:7 as a whole is that only those who rely on faith are Abraham's sons and daughters, i.e., his true heirs. In 2:16, Paul has already established that even Jewish Christians must be justified through faith in Christ and not through the works of the law. At 3:2, Paul also challenged the Galatian Christians to recognize the reality of their own experience: they had received the Spirit through "hearing of faith" rather than "works of the law." Galatians 3:7—4:7 provides additional arguments in support.

1. Only Those Who Rely on Faith Are Blessed Together with Believing Abraham (3:7–14)

Table 20: The Flow of 3:7–14				
Connector	At	Connects	With	Function
ἄρα	3:7	3:7–14	3:6	Infers (from 3:6)
δέ	3:8	3:8	3:7	Elaborates (to add support to 3:7)
ὥστε	3:9	3:9	3:8	Result
γάρ (2x)	3:10	3:10–12	3:9	Supports (with status of opposite group)
δέ	3:11	3:11	3:10	Elaborates (no one is justified before God by means of the law)
δέ	3:12	3:12	3:10–11	Elaborates (the law does not rely on faith)
Closely related concepts	3:13	3:13–14	3:10–12	Contrast (those Christ redeemed from the law's curse and those under its curse)
ἵνα (2x)	3:14	3:14	3:13	Purposes (tied to receiving Abraham's blessing [3:9] and the Spirit [3:2, 5] by faith)

Paul is confident that his audience already accepts the truth from Scripture that Abraham was counted righteous through faith. He reminds them that they already know a further logical consequence of this well-known fact:[16]

16. ἄρα introduces a consequence from 3:6 (Levinsohn, "Galatians," 316). In my view, 3:6 is connected to 3:1–5 through the syntactic subordination of the comparative clause introduced by καθώς to the implied answer ("it was by hearing with faith that God had supplied them with the Spirit and worked miracles among them") in 3:5. However, 3:5 is simultaneously the ground for the inferred consequence in 3:7

since faith was the path for Abraham, the father, it follows then (ἄρα) that only those who rely on faith are Abraham's sons and daughters.[17] In case this was not enough, Paul adds (δὲ) further support from Scripture. Indeed, because Scripture foresaw that God would justify the gentiles by faith, it proclaimed the good news beforehand to Abraham that "all nations would be blessed in you" (Gen 12:3; 18:18). Galatians 3:9 (ὥστε) reinforces the inference already drawn in 3:7.[18] In 3:7, those who rely on faith (i.e., those who believe) are sons and daughters of Abraham. In 3:9, they are blessed together with believing Abraham.[19]

The status of those who do not belong to this group supports (γὰρ) Paul's immediately preceding claim that only those who rely on faith experience blessing (3:7–9).[20] Perhaps shockingly to the Galatian churches, as many as rely on the works of the law are under a curse. Previous mentions of works of the law in opposition to faith in 3:2 and 3:5 already prepared the way for juxtaposing those who rely on works of the law with those who rely on faith.

1. Unapologetically, Paul makes it clear that as many as rely on the works of the law are, in fact, under a curse. We know this because (γὰρ) it is written in Scripture (Deut 27:26) that "cursed is everyone who does not remain in all the things written in the book of the law to do them" (3:10).[21]

2. Moreover (δὲ), the fact that no one is justified before God by means of the law is evident. This is because "the righteous shall live by faith" (3:11, citing Hab 2:4).

3. Furthermore (δὲ), the law does not rely on faith.

4. On the contrary (ἀλλ'), "the one who does these things shall live by them" (3:12, citing Lev 18:5).

(signaled by ἄρα). So, 3:5 is closely connected to both 3:1–5 and 3:7–14, but through different means.

17. While many interpret the verb as an exhortation, I agree with Longenecker (*Galatians*, 114) that it serves as a disclosure formula reminding the audience of what they already know. With Levinsohn ("Galatians," 317), I see this formula as giving prominence to the proposition that only those who rely on faith are Abraham's sons and daughters.

18. ὥστε introduces the conclusion of the 3:7–9 subunit (Levinsohn, "Galatians," 316).

19. The mention of Abraham "believing" (3:6) and the characterizing of Abraham as τῷ πιστῷ Ἀβραάμ (believing Abraham [3:7]) demonstrates that "those who rely on faith" means "those who believe."

20. Moo, *Galatians*, s.vv. "The Blessing of Abraham" (Gal 3:7–14).

21. This verse provides more support for the interpretation of "works of the law" so far. Relying on the works of the law is linked to doing all the things written in the book of the law. Similarly, Moo, *Galatians*, s.vv. "The Blessing of Abraham" (Gal 3:7–14).

The Scriptures are clear that those who do not continuously do what the law requires are cursed. What would lead to the premise that those who rely on the works of the law are under a curse? They do not fully meet the requirement of perfect obedience to the law![22] As a result, those who rely on faith are blessed, while those who rely on doing what the law requires are cursed.

In an abrupt contrast to those who rely on the law (who are under a curse) in v. 11, v. 13 proclaims that Christ has redeemed Paul and his audience from the curse of the law.[23] Christ did this by becoming a curse for us. We know this because it is written in Scripture (Deut 21:23) that "cursed is everyone who hangs on a tree" (3:13). The reference to hanging on a tree connects Christ's redemption from the curse of the law (by becoming a curse) to Christ's crucifixion (3:1).

Christ's purpose in redemption is so that "the blessing of Abraham might come through Christ Jesus to the gentiles." The language of blessing and gentiles connects back to 3:8, which notes that all nations would be blessed in Abraham, and 3:9, which states that those who rely on faith are blessed together with believing Abraham. A second purpose statement is: "So that we might receive the promised Spirit through faith." Receiving the blessing of Abraham is thus connected to receiving the promised Spirit.[24] This ties back to Paul's expected answers to his rhetorical questions in 3:2 and 3:5: the Galatians received the Spirit, and God supplied them with the Spirit through faith. So, the blessing of Abraham and the gift of the Spirit are also linked with both faith and Christ.[25] Moreover, redemption by becoming a curse for us ties to the law's curse (3:10) and Christ being crucified (3:1). So, while there is no conjunction linking 3:13–14 to 3:7–12, they belong together as one subunit. Galatians 3:13–14 is closely connected to 3:7–12 and brings to a close the themes of 3:7–14.[26]

In addition, Christ being crucified, in turn, connects with Christ giving himself for our sins. Therefore, a purpose previously expressed, namely, to rescue Paul and his audience from the present evil age (1:4) is also related

---

22. Similarly, Moo, *Galatians*, s.vv. "The Blessing of Abraham" (Gal 3:7–14). In my mind, the case of "works of the law" being identified as doing what the law requires is pretty airtight by this point as we interpret Galatians with Galatians.

23. Moo, *Galatians*, s.vv. "The Blessing of Abraham" (Gal 3:7–14); Schreiner, *Galatians*, 202.

24. Some witnesses read "the blessing associated with the Spirit" rather than "the promised associated with the Spirit." "Blessing" appears to be influenced by "the blessing of Abraham" earlier in the same verse. See Moo, *Galatians*, s.vv. "The Blessing of Abraham" (Gal 3:7–14), "Additional Notes."

25. Moo, *Galatians*, s.vv. "The Blessing of Abraham" (Gal 3:7–14).

26. Similarly, Levinsohn, "Galatians," 315. However, I do not think that it is helpful to claim a chiasm here.

to the two purposes here. In other words, receiving the promised Spirit is part of receiving the blessing of Abraham, which leads to (at least in part) being rescued from this present evil age. In addition, the fact that Christ had to be crucified to accomplish these things means that the blessing of Abraham and the gift of the Spirit cannot be obtained through works of the law. If the Galatians grasped the full significance of Christ crucified, they would not be so foolish as to be bewitched.

2. The Inheritance Does Not Rely on Law, but Rather on a Promise (3:15—4:7)

The next section begins (3:15–18) and ends (4:1–7) with a human analogy. The analogies are not the main points themselves. Instead, it is what the analogies help establish. The different points are tied together by the inheritance relying on a promise rather than law (3:18, 29; 4:5–7), given to those who believe (3:22).

A. THE LAW DOES NOT INVALIDATE A COVENANT ALREADY VALIDATED BY GOD (3:15–18)

Table 21: The Flow of 3:15–18

Connector	At	Connects	With	Function
None	3:15			Minor break
δὲ	3:16a	3:16	3:15	Elaborates (with lexical and conceptual repetition to tie back to 3:7–14)
Closely related concepts	3:16b	3:16b	3:16a	Defines (negates possible interpretation)
ἀλλ'	3:16c	3:16c–d	3:16b	Corrects (in contrast)
Relative clause	3:16d	3:16d	3:16c	Identifies
δὲ	3:17	3:17–18	3:15–16	Elaborates (on validity of God's promise)
γὰρ	3:18a	3:18	3:17	Supports (validity of God's promise)
δὲ	3:18b	3:18b	3:18a	Elaborates (by promise rather than law)

"Brothers and sisters" is one of the ways Paul typically addresses his audience. So, such an address is usually not that significant. However, in Galatians, he just characterized them as foolish Galatians (3:1) and expressed doubt about whether their experience of receiving the Spirit had been in vain (3:4). Furthermore, Paul appears to be moving towards more inclusive language already before v. 15: Christ redeemed "us" from the curse of the law (3:13) and so that "we" might receive the promised Spirit through faith (3:14).[27] Therefore, I believe that Paul is preparing the way for his direct plea to imitate him and live as he does in 4:12. He is subtly moving the audience to think of themselves as agreeing with him already.

Paul speaks at a human level (κατὰ ἄνθρωπον λέγω) and draws his audience's attention to an analogy with testamentary law. By using "validated" (κεκυρωμένην), Paul may imply the death of the person who made the testament (like in Heb 9:16). They could cancel or modify the testament during their lifetimes. However, the testament was validated only at their death. By then, they could no longer change it (being dead), and no one else was allowed to do so.[28] In any case, the point of Paul's analogy is clear: even human testaments were usually not meant to be annulled or added to.[29]

Paul elaborates (δὲ) that God's promises were spoken specifically to Abraham and Abraham's offspring. "Offspring" (σπέρμα) is a collective singular noun. In the book of Genesis, God promised Abraham land and blessing for the nations. The promises given to Abraham were also given specifically to his "offspring" (Gen 12:1–3; 15:1–5; 17:4–8; 18:18; 22:17–18). They were subsequently confirmed to Isaac (Gen 26:3–4) and Jacob (28:13–15; 35:11–12). Given these facts, one would expect "offspring" to refer to Jews, the physical descendants of Abraham.[30]

Instead, Paul notes that the Scripture does not say "and to offsprings" (καὶ τοῖς σπέρμασιν), as if referring to many, but as to one, "and to your offspring" (καὶ τῷ σπέρματί σου), who is Christ. Different explanations have been given as to how Paul could legitimately interpret the Scriptures as referring to a singular offspring who is Christ. It appears that Paul is well aware that "offspring" is a collective noun that can refer to a single descendant or multiple descendants. In the first instance, he identifies the referent as a single descendant, Christ. It is through Christ that the promised blessing was to come to all the gentiles. In the second instance, the reference is to all who receive this blessing. Indeed, Paul explicitly includes all who belong

---

27. See further table 4, "First-Person Plural References."
28. Bruce, *Galatians*, 170.
29. DeSilva, *Galatians*, 308.
30. Schreiner, *Galatians*, 227–28.

to Christ as Abraham's offspring (τοῦ Ἀβραὰμ σπέρμα) in 3:29.[31] Paul may be reading the Genesis promises in light of the storyline of the Old Testament, which narrows the promised offspring down to a son of David, which then finds its fulfillment in Jesus Christ.[32] In any case, his point is that the promise belongs to Christ in the first instance.

After establishing that even human testaments could not be annulled or added to once validated and that the promises were spoken to Abraham and his singular offspring Christ (3:15–16), Paul highlights his next point (δὲ) with a forward-pointing reference: "This I say."[33] After putting together the necessary background, Paul gets to his main point for 3:15–18. Paul recasts the promise as a covenant (διαθήκην) already validated (προκεκυρωμένην) by God. The law, which came 430 years later, does not invalidate (ἀκυροῖ) it, which would result in nullifying (καταργῆσαι) the promise (3:17).

Besides the promise coming first, why is it that the law cannot annul it or add to it? This is because the inheritance relies on a promise that God graciously gave to Abraham. Instead of spelling this answer out directly, Paul poses a nonfactual condition: for (γὰρ) if the inheritance (κληρονομία) relies on law, then it no longer relies on a promise. So, the inheritance does not rely on the law, but instead on a promise. Moreover (δὲ), God graciously gave the inheritance to Abraham through a promise (3:18).

B. THE LAW CONFINES ALL UNDER SIN IN SERVICE OF THE PROMISE (3:19–22)

Table 22: The Flow of 3:19–22				
Connector	At	Connects	With	Function
οὖν	3:19a	3:19–22	3:15–18	Infers (question arising from 3:15–18)
Answer to question	3:19b	3:19b–c	3:19a	Answers (question in 3:19a)
Relative clause	3:19c	3:19c	3:19b	Describes limitations
δὲ (2x)	3:20	3:20	3:19c	Elaborates
οὖν	3:21a	3:21–22	3:19b–20	Infers (question arising from 3:19b–20)

---

31. Bruce, *Galatians*, 172.

32. Schreiner, *Galatians*, 229–30.

33. Levinsohn notes that "this" and "I say" gives prominence to what follows ("Galatians," 318).

γάρ	3:21c	3:21c-22	3:21b	Supports (3:21b denial of 3:21a question)
ἀλλά	3:22a	3:22	3:21c	Corrects (in contrast)
ἵνα	3:22b	3:22b	3:22a	Purpose (promise given by faith)

At this point, Paul has clarified the roles the law does not play. A natural question arises: What role then (οὖν) does it play? Paul proceeds to articulate his audience's potential question and answer it: Why, then, the law?[34] It was added on account of transgression.[35] There is a time limitation: until the offspring to whom the promise was given should come. Paul also adds a description of how the law came: It had been ordained through angels by the hands of a mediator (3:19). What any of these things mean is not yet clear at this point in Paul's discourse. If we patiently read on, most (though not all) questions will be answered.

The very next verse is somewhat cryptic: now (δέ) the mediator is not for one party, but (δέ) God is one (3:20). Several pieces of evidence within the context may help us piece together the main idea: the law came only later (3:17), is temporary (3:19), and cannot annul or add to the promise (3:15-17). God also graciously gave the promise to Abraham specifically (3:18). Paul added a description of the law as ordained through angels by the hands of a mediator before talking further about the mediator. This suggests that v. 20 involves another way the law is inferior to the promise. It seems, then, that the point is that the law is inferior to the promise because it needs mediation. God ordained it for the people through angels by the hands of a mediator. By contrast, the one God had spoken the promise directly to Abraham.[36]

Another natural question that may arise is whether the law is at odds with God's promises.[37] Paul again articulates his audience's potential question and answers it: Is the law then (οὖν) against the promises? Paul's answer is an emphatic no. He could have directly explained that a law capable of giving life had not been given. Instead, he underlines this point by positing a hypothetical scenario: if a law capable of giving life had been given, then

---

34. The rhetorical questions in 3:19 and 3:21 both introduce a new aspect of a subject, drawing an inference (both introduced by οὖν) from the preceding discussion. See Beekman and Callow, *Translating Word of God*, 245-46.

35. Asking the question rhetorically and then answering it makes the answer prominent (Levinsohn, "Galatians," 318).

36. Similarly, Schreiner, *Galatians*, 243.

37. τοῦ θεοῦ is absent in two important witnesses. "Of God" makes the referent more explicit, but the promises of God are meant regardless. See Moo, *Galatians*, s.vv. "The Law in Salvation History" (Gal 3:15-25), "Additional Notes."

righteousness would have truly been by the law (3:21).³⁸ Since we already know that the law does not bring righteousness (2:16, 21; 3:11), we know we do not have a law capable of giving life.³⁹

In contrast to this untrue scenario, the correct scenario is that the Scripture shut in (συνέκλεισεν) all under sin (3:22). This is the main point of 3:19–22. So, the law does have a positive role to play. Besides correcting a potential false conclusion, it elaborates that confining all under sin was part of what was involved in "added on account of transgression" (3:19). In addition, the purpose of Christ's redemption of Paul and his audience from the curse of the law and the purpose of this confinement also seem closely related:

1. So that we might receive the promised Spirit through faith (3:14)

2. So that the promise might be given by means of faith in Jesus Christ to those who believe (3:22)⁴⁰

If we are right to make this connection, Scripture confines all under sin and places all under a curse for failing to obey perfectly. Furthermore, the law functions in this way in service of the promise to ensure that it can be received only through faith.

C. The Law Serves as a Guardian, Directing to Christ as the Destination (3:23–29)

Table 23: The Flow of 3:23–29				
Connector	At	Connects	With	Function
δέ	3:23	3:23–29	3:15–22	Elaborates (situation before faith)
ὥστε	3:24a	3:24	3:23	Result (supported by 3:23)
ἵνα	3:24b	3:24b	3:24a	Purpose (justified by faith)
δέ	3:25	3:25–29	3:23–24	Elaborates (situation after faith)

---

38. There are several textual variants that appear to come from scribal confusion of ἄν and ἦν, ἐκ and ἐν. No significance difference in interpretation results. See Betz, *Galatians*, 173.

39. Similarly, Moo, *Galatians*, s.vv. "The Law in Salvation History" (Gal 3:15–25). Yoon points out that Paul posing a false scenario involving the law giving life implies that the contention over the law was about more than being a boundary marker ("Transitivity Network," 94).

40. Given what we have seen so far, we would naturally read Paul as saying that God's promises are given to those who believe by means of faith in Christ Jesus. Similarly, Moo, *Galatians*, s.vv. "The Law in Salvation History" (Gal 3:15–25).

γὰρ	3:26	3:26–29	3:25	Supports (change after faith)
γὰρ	3:27	3:27–29	3:26	Supports (status as God's children)
3 negated pairs	3:28a–c	3:28	3:27	Redefines
γὰρ	3:28d	3:28d–29	3:28a–c	Supports (negating distinctions in three pairs)
δὲ	3:29	3:29	3:28d	Elaborates (status as Abraham's heirs)

Moreover (δὲ), before this faith came, Paul and his audience were held in custody (ἐφρουρούμεθα) by the law. They were shut in (συγκλειόμενοι) with the faith about to be revealed in view (3:23). Paul designates the entire period before Christ's coming as "before faith came."[41] The temporary role of the law was previously mentioned in 3:19: "added until the offspring to whom the promise was given should come." The role of the law in holding in custody and confining is likewise temporary here, applying to before faith came. So, it is not the case that the law is at odds with the promises (false scenario rejected in 3:21). The correct conclusion (ὥστε) is that the law has become Paul's and his audience's guardian with a view to Christ as their destination.[42] This is the main point of 3:23–29. The purpose is that they might be justified by faith (3:24).[43] Moreover (δὲ), after faith came, Paul and his audience were no longer under this guardian (3:25).[44]

How can this be? Paul explains (γὰρ) that all members of his audience are sons and daughters of God through faith in Christ Jesus (3:26).[45] He

---

41. Schreiner, *Galatians*, 245.

42. Similarly, Levinsohn identifies 3:24 as the conclusion that answers the question of 3:21 ("Galatians," 318).

43. The same action of "shutting in" (συγκλείω) and the same purpose involving faith as the means ties together 3:22 and 3:24. Consequently, being justified by faith (3:24) is connected with the promise being given by means of faith in Jesus Christ to those who believe (3:22).

44. In the context, no longer being under this guardian involves no longer being held in custody and confined. If we rely purely on the context of the text, holding in custody and confinement would seem to be the primary functions of this guardian. Hong (*Law in Galatians*, 160) and Martyn (*Galatians*, 363) similarly emphasize these functions of παιδαγωγὸς.

45. It is uncertain whether "through faith in Christ Jesus" should be read as explicitly specifying Christ as the object of "faith" here. I lean towards this interpretation because "faith" is used absolutely in 3:23–25 and an explicit association of this faith with Christ as "faith in Christ Jesus" is my first interpretation when reading through the text. If Paul wanted to avoid this interpretation, he could easily have changed up the

elaborates further (γὰρ) that as many of them as have been baptized into Christ have put on Christ as one would put on clothes (3:27). The implications that Paul draws are that former distinctions between Jew and Greek, slave and free, male and female become irrelevant in Christ. Gentiles are heirs alongside Jews, slaves together with those who are free, and women as well as men. This is because (γὰρ) they are all one in Christ Jesus (3:28). Furthermore (δὲ), if they belong to Christ,[46] then (ἄρα) they are Abraham's offspring, i.e., heirs according to promise (κατ' ἐπαγγελίαν κληρονόμοι [3:29]). It appears that being baptized into Christ, having put on Christ, being one in Christ Jesus, and belonging to Christ are different ways of portraying the same reality of union with Christ. Tying back to 3:7-9, Paul reaffirms that only those who rely on faith and thus belong to Christ are Abraham's offspring. It is only through faith in Christ that they have this status. As Abraham's offspring, they are the heirs who will inherit Abraham's blessing, which relies on God's promise.[47]

D. Believers Are No Longer Slaves Under the Law, but Rather Sons and Thus Heirs (4:1–7)

Table 24: The Flow of 4:1–7				
Connector	At	Connects	With	Function
δέ	4:1	4:1–7	3:15–29	Elaborates (on status of heirs)
ἀλλ'	4:2	4:2	4:1	Corrects (expectations in contrast to reality)
οὕτως καί	4:3	4:3	4:1–2	Compares (to analogy of underage heir)
δὲ	4:4	4:4–5	4:1–3	Elaborates (on change in situation)
ἵνα (2x)	4:5	4:5	4:4	Purposes (why God changed the situation)
δέ	4:6	4:6	4:1–5	Elaborates (further on what God changed)

word order to put "in Christ Jesus" before "through faith." He did not do so. Regardless, my interpretation does not rely on this disputable point, which I hold loosely.

46. The immediate context makes clear that this condition is true—since they are all one in Christ Jesus (3:28), obviously they belong to Christ. Similarly, Nicolle, "Conditionals in Galatians," 103.

47. Similarly, Schreiner, *Galatians*, 259.

ὥστε	4:7a	4:7a	4:1–6	Result (changed status)
ἀλλ'	4:7b	4:7b	4:7a	Corrects (expectations in contrast to reality)

How does Paul continue after building such a robust case that it is only through faith in Christ that the Galatians become heirs of Abraham's blessing? Starting with the words "now I say" (λέγω δέ),[48] Paul returns to and builds on the analogy he introduced in 3:23–25 about living under the authority of a guardian (παιδαγωγὸς).[49] Notably, the context of the guardianship has shifted to the guardianship of an heir specifically. The focus on heirs picks up from 3:29, which describes Abraham's offspring as heirs.[50] The spotlight also turns from the guardian's authority to the heir's experience (i.e., the one under the guardian's authority).[51] This is accomplished by introducing the plight of the heir first before mentioning the guardians: as long as an heir is a minor, he[52] is no different from a slave, even though he is master of all (4:1). Paul portrays the heir's life as resembling more that of a slave, even though he simultaneously holds the title to the entire estate.[53] Instead (ἀλλ') of living as the master of the estate, the heir lives under the supervision of "guardians" (ἐπιτρόπους) and "managers" (οἰκονόμους). This situation lasts until it is time for him to gain his inheritance. That time is determined by his father (4:2).

Paul explicitly compares the situation of his audience with this analogy using the words "thus also" (οὕτως καί). When they were minors (i.e., before they received their inheritance), Paul and his audience were also

---

48. Levinsohn points out that δέ indicates that 4:1 starts the next step of the argument begun in 3:15. The following evidence supports seeing a new subunit at 4:1: "I say," the initial situational frame "as long as the heir is a child," and the change from second to third person ("Galatians," 319).

49. Similarly, Levinsohn, "Galatians," 319. Moo has a nice table showing the connections between 3:23–29 and 4:1–7 (*Galatians*, s.vv. "From Slaves to Sons of God" [Gal 4:1–7]).

50. Levinsohn observes that "the final word of the subsection is κληρονόμοι 'heirs,' which has been postposed to provide a hook in anticipation of ὁ κληρονόμος 'the heir' becoming thematic in 4:1" ("Galatians," 318).

51. Runge, *Galatians*, Gal 3:19–29.

52. I am using a masculine pronoun "he" only here in the analogy about heirs because Paul is using an everyday analogy from the world he knew. Back then heirs were usually males. Paul's statement that males and females are heirs together (3:28–29) would have been radical in his day.

53. DeSilva, *Galatians*, 346.

enslaved to the elements of the world (τὰ στοιχεῖα τοῦ κόσμου), which include the law (4:3).[54]

Now (δέ) those days are over. When the fullness of time came, God sent his Son to redeem those under the authority of the law (4:4–5).[55] Notably, God's Son is described as being born of a woman and born under the law. Paul wants his audience to think of Christ and his redemptive work in those terms. God's Son was born a human and thus shared their humanity. He also was born under the authority of the law and thus shared the obligation to fulfill it.[56] This ties back to 3:13, where Christ's redemption of those under the law involved Christ coming under the law's curse. It also sheds light on 2:19: Christ came under the law's curse when he was crucified. As those crucified together with Christ, in a sense, those who belong to Christ also came under the law's curse and died on the cross. This would explain what Paul meant by "I, through the law, died to the law."

God's Son redeemed those under the law, which included Paul and the Jewish people (though perhaps not his gentile audience in the first instance), so that they might receive adoption as sons (υἱοθεσίαν).[57] In other words, God's Son liberated and freed those who were enslaved under the law, so that believers could become God's sons (4:4–5). This appears to be related to 3:13–14, which parallels 4:4–5 with similar statements about redemption for those under the law's curse.[58]

In 3:13–14, redemption results in receiving the promised Spirit through faith. Galatians 4:6 similarly mentions God giving the Spirit. Furthermore (δέ), since they are sons,[59] God sent the Spirit of his Son into their hearts.[60]

---

54. Even though others things may be included, Paul clearly applies the term to the law primarily in this context.

55. The fullness of time in 4:4 corresponds to the time fixed by God the Father in the analogy about fathers fixing the time an heir gained his inheritance (Bruce, *Galatians*, 194).

56. Longenecker, *Galatians*, 171–72.

57. It is unclear if Paul includes gentiles in some sense among those under the law. However, Christ redeeming those under the law results in Paul's audience of mainly gentile Galatian Christians likewise becoming sons and thus heirs.

58. Moo, *Galatians*, s.vv. "From Slaves to Sons of God" (Gal 4:1–7).

59. Back then heirs were usually males. I used "sons" here as there is an intentional connection between having the status as sons and having the Spirit of God's Son into their hearts. Of course, Paul applied this status to both men and women. So, it would be appropriate to translate "sons" as "sons and daughters." The downside would be potentially overlooking the link between "sons" and "Son" and underappreciating the radicalness of multitudes of both women and men gaining the status of a male heir in Paul's world.

60. The manuscripts tradition varies between "your" (second-person plural) and "our" (first-person plural) hearts. One would expect "your." "Our" is unexpected and more likely to be corrected to "your." See Moo, *Galatians*, s.vv. "From Slaves to Sons of

Within their hearts, this Spirit addresses God boldly and intimately as their dear Father (4:6). This is the evidence that they are truly God's children. "Therefore" (ὥστε), collectively, they are no longer slaves but sons. And if they are sons, they are heirs through God (4:7).[61] This is the main point of 4:1–7.

They already know that they are sons. After all, v. 6 already says, "because they are sons." Moreover, v. 7 starts by inferring that they are no longer slaves but sons. It is clear, then, that they are heirs.[62] God made them heirs by sending his Son.

To recap, 3:7—4:7 provides the following overall picture: Those whom God's Son has redeemed from under the law are adopted as God's sons. This was accomplished through Christ being crucified. What they inherit as sons are the blessing of Abraham and the promised Spirit. All these are included in the inheritance promised to Abraham and Abraham's offspring. The true sons and daughters of Abraham receive these through faith in Christ. By contrast, the law does not give life and brings only slavery. It is only when the Galatians recognize these tightly connected facts that they fully appreciate the significance of the crucified Christ. However, once they realize these things, the Galatians would better appreciate that their experience of receiving the Spirit through believing what they heard rather than doing what the law requires is well founded. They would agree with Paul's characterization that letting anyone bewitch them into relying on doing what the law requires would be foolish.

God" (Gal 4:1–7), "Additional Notes."

61. The other textual variants here are best explained if "through God" is the original reading. See Bruce, *Galatians*, 200–201.

62. Similarly, Nicolle, "Conditionals in Galatians," 103.

GALATIANS 4:8–31

OUTLINE

II. First Round of Rebuke, Backed by Extended Support (1:6—2:21)

III. Second Round of Rebuke, Backed by Extended Support (3:1—4:7)

IV. Third Round of Rebuke (4:8–31)

    A. It Is Inconceivable for the Galatians to Return to Weak and Poor Elements (4:8–11)

    B. Become Like Paul, Just as Paul Had Become Like the Galatian Christians (4:12–20)

    C. Call to Listen to the Law and Recognize That They Are Children of the Free Woman, Children of Promise Like Isaac (4:21–31)

IV. THIRD ROUND OF REBUKE (4:8–31)

MY ANALYSIS OF HOW 4:8–11 fits in the larger structure differs significantly from most commentators.[1] This is because I see 4:8–31 as a third round of rebuke. Why did I identify this section in this way? The primary criterion for making this determination is the shift from exposition back to rebuke. In addition, the first part of 4:8–9 summarizes 3:7—4:7, effectively allowing that section to ground this next round of rebuke. At the highest level of the discourse, I see three main points so far after the letter opening:

---

1. Moo comes closest to my interpretation. He sees a fundamental shift from argument (3:7—4:7) to appeal (4:8–31) (*Galatians*, s.vv. "Appeal" [Gal 4:8–31]).

1. I am astonished that you are so quickly turning away from the divine gospel brought to you by a divinely appointed servant of Christ.
2. O foolish Galatians, I want to learn from you whether you received the Spirit through doing what the law requires or through hearing accompanied by faith.
3. How can you return again to the weak and poor elements?

Table 25: Overview of the Flow of 4:8–31				
Connector	At	Connects	With	Function
Ἀλλά	4:8	4:8–11	3:1—4:7	Corrects (starts third-round rebuke)
None	4:12	4:12–20	4:8–11	Minor break. Switch to exhortation (become law free like Paul)
None	4:21	4:21–31	4:12–20	Minor break. Switch to challenging (based on the law)

How exactly does Paul resume his rebuke? Like in 3:1–5, this round of rebuke uses rhetorical questions to challenge the Galatians and reveals Paul's unfavorable appraisals of them. The rhetorical questions confront the Galatians in the following ways:

1. Not to return to weak and poor elements in light of all they already know and have experienced (4:8–9)
2. To rethink their unfavorable change in opinion of Paul and to recognize that he has not become their enemy by speaking the truth to them (4:15–16)
3. To listen to the law (4:21)

The negative assessments are revealed by:

1. Paul's fear about whether his ministry to them had been in vain (4:11)
2. His great concern for them and inability to change his tone (4:20)

To take a larger view, I see the mainline of this third round of rebuke in 4:8–31 proceeding in the following way:

1. 4:8–11: It Is Inconceivable for the Galatians to Return to Weak and Poor Elements
2. 4:12–20: Become Like Paul, Just as Paul Had Become Like the Galatian Christians

3. 4:21–31: Call to Listen to the Law and Recognize That They Are Children of the Free Woman, Children of Promise Like Isaac

A. It Is Inconceivable for the Galatians to Return to Weak and Poor Elements (4:8–11)

Table 26: The Flow of 4:8–11				
Connector	At	Connects	With	Function
Ἀλλά	4:8	4:8–11	3:1—4:7	Corrects (and uses lexical and conceptual repetition to summarize 3:7—4:7 to set the stage; starts third round of rebuke)
Closely related concept	4:10	4:10	4:8–9	Specific evidence
Closely related concept	4:11	4:11	4:8–10	Response (negative appraisal)

Paul moves from exposition (3:7—4:7) back to rebuke in 4:8–11.[2] Galatians 4:8–9 functions together rhetorically, forming a then-now contrast.[3] The extended "then" part summarizes 4:1–7 in particular (and, by extension, 3:7—4:7) to set the stage for the next round of rebuke.[4] As a brief recap. Paul has argued from Scripture and analogies from everyday life to establish that only those who rely on faith are Abraham's true heirs. In 3:7–14, he established that only those who rely on faith are blessed together with believing Abraham. This is because as many as rely on the works of the law are under a curse (3:10–12) while Christ has redeemed them from the curse of the law (3:13–14). In 3:15—4:7, he proved that the inheritance does not rely on the law but on God's promise. As he explained:

---

2. Similarly Moo, *Galatians*, s.vv. "Appeal" (4:8–31).
3. Runge, *Galatians*, Gal 4:1–11.
4. Moo argues similarly that "the imagery of 4:1–7 brings to a climax some of the key themes of 3:7-4:7 as a whole: the inability of the law to secure Abrahamic inheritance (3:6–9, 14, 15–18; cf. the connection of 'heir' in 4:1, 7 with Abraham via 3:29); the consequent need for redemption from the curse of the law (3:13; 4:5); the pre-Christian state as one of bondage to the law (3:22–25; 'under the law' in 4:5); and the gift of sonship in Christ (3:26; 4:5–7). Therefore, as the initial paragraph in Paul's appeal to the Galatians, 4:8-11 applies the wider argument of which 4:1–7 is the conclusion" (*Galatians*, s.vv. "Appeal" [Gal 4:8–31]).

1. 3:15–18: The Law Does Not Invalidate a Covenant Already Validated by God
2. 3:19–22: The Law Confines All Under Sin in Service of the Promise
3. 3:23–29: The Law Serves as a Guardian, Directing to Christ as the Destination[5]
4. 4:1–7: Believers Are No Longer Slaves Under the Law, but Rather Sons and Thus Heirs

Nevertheless (Ἀλλά), even though they know all of this (3:7—4:7) and it matches their personal experience of receiving the Spirit through faith (3:2), Paul must resume challenging them with a rhetorical question: How can they return again to the weak and poor elements to which they desire to be enslaved again (4:9)? This is the main point of 4:8–11 and 4:8–31 as a whole. This recalls their past predicament of being enslaved to the elements of the world (4:3). On the one hand, the situation back then (τότε μὲν) was that formerly, when they did not know God, they were enslaved to what are not gods by nature (4:8).[6] On the other hand, the situation now (νῦν δὲ) is that they know God or rather are known by God (4:9). Given the dramatic difference between then and now, why in the world are they turning back? It is inconceivable for them to do so!

The specific example Paul cites to back up his accusation that they are returning to serve the weak and poor elements[7] is as follows: you are observing days and months and seasons and years (4:10).[8] These most likely refer to sacred days of the Jewish religious calendar.[9] Closing with yet another negative appraisal, Paul expresses his fear for them lest somehow he might have worked in vain (4:11). In presenting his gospel message to the Jerusalem apostles (to avoid potentially being undermined by those held in high esteem), Paul expressed a similar concern to prevent any possibility that he was running or had run in vain (2:2). Here the Galatians' own situation is at stake, if indeed their experiences had been in vain (3:4), and Paul's ministry to them had been in vain (4:11).

---

5. Levinsohn's analysis of 3:15–18, 19–22, 23–29 is similar ("Galatians," 318).
6. Paul closely links the weak and poor elements and what are not gods by nature.
7. Longenecker, *Galatians*, 181–82.
8. Yoon points out that this shows that Paul was concerned about observing other elements of the Jewish law and not just about circumcision ("Transitivity Network," 95).
9. DeSilva, *Galatians*, 366–67.

B. Become Like Paul, Just as Paul Had Become Like the Galatian Christians (4:12–20)

Table 27: The Flow of 4:12-20				
Connector	At	Connects	With	Function
None	4:12	4:12–20	4:8–11	Minor break. Switch to exhortation (become law free like Paul)
δέ	4:13	4:13–14	4:12	Elaborates (on circumstances)
καί	4:14a	4:14a–b	4:13	Associated responses (negated expectations)
ἀλλ'	4:14c	4:14c	4:14a–b	Corrects (expectations)
οὖν	4:15a	4:15a	4:12b–14	Infers (expectation of persistent positive response)
γάρ	4:15b	4:15b	4:15a	Supports (expectation)
ὥστε	4:16	4:16	4:15	Result (questions false perception)
Closely related concept	4:17a	4:17a	4:16	Negate positive appraisal
ἀλλ'	4:17b	4:17b–c	4:17a	Corrects (with negative appraisal in contrast)
δέ	4:18	4:18	4:17	Elaborates (on proper parameters)
δέ	4:20a	4:19–20	4:17–18	Elaborates (on Paul's desires)

After floating the possibility that his ministry to them might somehow have been for nothing, Paul makes an impassioned plea. This is Paul's first direct appeal. It is the main point of 4:12–20, even though Paul will quickly return to rebuke.[10] He supports his plea by addressing them afresh as "brothers and sisters." In a context immediately after expressing his exasperation with them (4:10–11), this address strategically fosters a sense of connection and kinship.[11] Paul reinforces his appeal to his brothers and sisters to become like him by begging them (4:12).[12]

---

10. He only returns to direct appeal in 5:1, but 5:1–15 is also overshadowed by rebuke. Extended appeal only commences at 5:16 and goes through 6:10.

11. DeSilva, *Galatians*, 377.

12 "I beg you" reinforces and gives prominence to this preceding appeal (Levinsohn, "Galatians," 322).

What does Paul mean by becoming like him? Galatians 2:19–21, which shared Paul's first-person experience, comes to mind: "For through the law I died to the law so that I might live to God. I have been crucified together with Christ. I no longer live, but Christ lives in me. And the life I now live in the flesh, I live by faith in the Son of God, who loved me and gave himself for me. I do not reject the grace of God. For if righteousness comes through the law, then Christ died for nothing." In 3:7—4:7, Paul has already largely explained what he means by these short and somewhat cryptic statements. Moreover, Paul has been using inclusive language to start to move the Galatians to agree with him: "Christ redeemed 'us' from the curse of the law" (3:13) and "so that 'we' might receive the promised Spirit through faith" (3:14). Before this faith came, "we" were held in custody by the law (3:23). The law has become "our" guardian with Christ as the destination. The purpose is that "we" might be justified by faith (3:24). Moreover (δὲ), after faith came, "we" are no longer under this guardian (3:25).[13] So, by becoming like Paul, the Galatians would likewise not reject the grace of God (2:21). They would agree with Paul that Christ did not die for nothing.

Besides calling the Galatians to become like him, Paul also grounds his appeal on his having become like them (4:12). In what sense had Paul become like them? Cephas, despite being a Jew, really lived like a gentile and not like a Jew. While Cephas started acting hypocritically by not behaving consistently with the truth of the gospel (2:14), Paul, the person who opposed and rebuked him, stayed true. Cephas and Paul were born Jews (Jews by nature) and not sinners from the gentiles (2:15). Because no one can be justified by the works of the law, even Jewish Christians must be justified through faith in Christ and not through the works of the law (2:16). If Paul (and Cephas, and other Jews involved in the mission to the gentiles) are not found to be sinners because they no longer keep the works of the law (2:17–18), then the Galatian churches likewise should become like Paul. Just as Paul through the law died to the law, so that he might live to God (2:19), the Galatian Christians should also become like Paul (4:12).

With the focus shifting to how Paul became like them, Paul continues to draw on the Galatians' personal relationship with him. They did him no wrong in the past (4:12). Furthermore (δὲ), they share common knowledge (as in 2:16) with Paul.[14] In this case, it surrounds the circumstances when Paul formerly preached the gospel to them. He did so because of weakness in the flesh (4:13). Paul was apparently sick in some way that was noticeable

---

13. See table 4, "First-Person Plural References."

14. As Levinsohn notes, "you know" gives prominence to the things Paul says the Galatians know ("Galatians," 322).

to the Galatians. In some sense, Paul's illness caused circumstances that led to or allowed Paul to proclaim the gospel. Despite Paul's illness, which could be seen as a sign that his message was not from God, the Galatians passed the test back then.[15] They neither scorned nor spat in response to the trial they endured in Paul's flesh.[16] Instead (ἀλλ'), they received Paul as if he were an angel of God, as if he were Christ Jesus himself (4:14). Paul likens their response to what they might have shown if an angel of God or even Christ Jesus himself had appeared to proclaim the good news to them.[17]

Next, Paul challenges the Galatian churches to rethink how they have gone away from their earlier pronouncement that Paul was a person specially favored by God: What happened, then (οὖν), to your earlier pronouncement of blessing?[18] Paul expected this blessing to persist because (γὰρ) he could offer solemn testimony of how great their former regard for him was.[19] Were it possible (and it was not),[20] they would have plucked out their own eyes and given them to him (4:15).[21] In a genuine sense, Paul should not have had to devote a whole section to prove that he is a servant of Christ and proclaims a divine rather than human gospel (1:10—2:21).

Given the turn of events, it is evident that the Galatians' former regard for Paul did not persist. So then (ὥστε), in their estimation, has Paul become their enemy by speaking the truth to them (4:16)?[22] In Paul's line of rhetorical questioning, he expects the Galatians to admit in their hearts that they should have continued to trust Paul as God's servant and Paul's message as God's message. They would acknowledge that Paul is not their enemy and

---

15. DeSilva, *Galatians*, 380.

16. As Yoon notes, τῇ σαρκί (the flesh) is an elliptical reference to ἀσθένειαν τῆς σαρκὸς (weakness in the flesh) in the previous verse ("Discourse Analysis and Metafunction," 107).

17. Aorist tense verb forms carry forward this brief narrative support material.

18. DeSilva, *Galatians*, 381; Moo, *Galatians*, s.vv. "Appeal" (Gal 4:8–31). What Beekman and Callow say about rhetorical questions that function as a statement of evaluation seems particularly on target here: "Judgments are made of the propriety, ethics, or value of an action, state, person, or thing, and such judgments are usually accompanied with emotional overtones and frequently imply an obligation on the part of the hearers to respond with appropriate action. It would seem that the question form is used as a more polite or less direct way to administer the rebuke or command" (*Translating Word of God*, 243).

19. As Levinsohn notes, "I testify to you" gives prominence to Paul's following assertion ("Galatians," 322).

20. Nicolle, "Conditionals in Galatians," 103–4.

21. It is possible that this statement confirms that Paul's illness had to do with some form of eye malady. However, this may also just be a vivid way to express something along the lines of "you would give your right arm for me."

22. As Yoon notes, the perfect tense form (stative aspect) γέγονα (I have become) is prominent ("Discourse Analysis and Metafunction," 108).

that he is speaking the truth when he rebukes them. He had given them no cause to change their opinion of him. Instead, Paul has consistently spoken and acted in accordance with the truth (2:5, 14). Just as he defended the truth at Antioch to preserve it for the developing mission to the gentiles, so also he is bringing the truth to the Galatians,[23]

After addressing the negative turn in sentiment towards him, Paul proceeds to discredit his opponents. This is similar to how he undermined the other gospel his opponents proclaimed (1:6–7) and pronounced his opponents cursed (1:8–9). It is also akin to how he painted his opponents in Jerusalem as "false brothers" who had sneaked in and slipped in as spies to enslave Christians (2:4). Paul accuses his rivals of selfish motives: "They are not zealous for you in a good way. Instead [ἀλλ'], they wish to shut you out, so that you might be zealous for them" (4:17).[24] We already know that they desire to distort the gospel of Christ (1:7). Later, Paul will portray them as wanting to make a good showing in the flesh (6:12) and to have the Galatians circumcised so that they could boast in their flesh (6:13). They want to shut the Galatians out (ἐκκλεῖσαι), so that the Galatians will zealously follow them (4:17). This is in contrast to the Scriptures, which accomplish God's noble purposes. The Scriptures shut in (συνέκλεισεν) all under sin so that the promise might be given by means of faith in Jesus Christ to those who believe (3:22). The Scriptures shut them in (συγκλειόμενοι) with the faith about to be revealed in view (3:23).

Now (δὲ) Paul would want the Galatians to show zeal for what is good all the time and not just while he is present with them (4:18).[25] That is, unfortunately, not the situation at hand. At 4:19, Paul addresses his audience directly again as "my children" (τέκνα μου).[26] He describes himself as a mother in childbirth: "My children, for whom I am once again in the pains of childbirth until Christ is formed in you."[27] Paul reveals his deep affection for and investment in the Galatian churches. He gave birth to them, and they are his dear children. The process of Christ being formed in them was in jeopardy. Paul is in agony. As he writes, his message is designed to get his children back on track. Moreover (δὲ), Paul wished he could be present with

---

23. Similarly, DeSilva, *Galatians*, 382–83.

24. As Yoon notes, different forms of the verb ζηλόω occur three times and form cohesive ties in 4:17–18 ("Textual Metafunction," 107).

25. As Yoon notes, the repeat of the verb παρεῖναι (to be present) links 4:18 with 4:20 ("Discourse Analysis and Metafunction," 107).

26. It is uncertain whether τέκνον or its diminutive form τεκνίον (perhaps adding more of a nuance of little or dear than τέκνον might on its own) should be read here.

27. The idea of Christ being formed in believers is likely related to Paul's assertion that Christ lives in him (2:20).

them even then and change his tone. This was because he was at a loss where they were concerned (4:20). Paul highlights his desire to deal differently with his dear friends in Galatia. He did not want to adopt a harsh tone in his letter. He emphasizes how his concern for them is the reason (ὅτι) for his stern message. It is also why he desires to be present with them and adopt a more affectionate tone. The circumstances, however, dictated otherwise. By stressing his deep affection for the Galatians and his desire for their good, Paul keeps his audience receptive to his message.[28]

C. Call to Listen to the Law and Recognize That They Are Children of the Free Woman, Children of Promise Like Isaac (4:21–31)

Table 28: The Flow of 4:21–31				
Connector	At	Connects	With	Function
None	4:21	4:21–31	4:8–20	Minor break. Switches to challenging (based on the law)
γὰρ	4:22	4:22–27	4:21	Supports (challenge using Pentateuch)
ἀλλ'	4:23	4:23–27	4:22	Corrects (perceptions)
Relative clause	4:24a	4:24a	4:22–23	Defines (as an allegory)
γάρ	4:24b	4:24b–27	4:24a	Supports (allegory)
μὲν	4:24c	4:24c–25	4:26	Contrast (present Jerusalem with 4:26)
δὲ	4:26a	4:26	4:24c–25	Contrast (Jerusalem above with 4:24c–25)
Relative clause	4:26b	4:26b	4:26a	Redefines (Jerusalem above as mother)
γάρ	4:27	4:27	4:26b	Supports (redefinition as mother)
δέ	4:28	4:28–31	4:21–27	Elaborates (on which group Galatians are in)

28. Similarly, DeSilva, *Galatians*, 387–88.

ἀλλ'	4:29	4:29	4:28	Corrects (perceptions about opponents)
ἀλλά	4:30	4:30	4:29	Corrects (perception about Scripture)
διό	4:31	4:31	4:21–30	Infers (from 4:21–30)

It becomes clear that Paul cannot significantly alter his tone. He returns to directly challenging his audience: Tell me . . . do you not listen to the law? He describes his audience as those who want to be under the law.[29] The implication is that his audience would not want to be under the law if they did listen to the law (4:21).[30] They should already know better from the things Paul previously referenced from the law:

1. "Cursed is everyone who does not remain in all the things written in the book of the law to do them." (Gal 3:10, citing Deut 27:26)

2. "The one who does these things shall live by them." (Gal 3:12, citing Lev 18:5)

So, what else can the Galatians learn from listening to the law? Paul adds further support here (γάρ). It is written in Scripture that Abraham had two sons, one from the slave woman and one from the free woman. However (ἀλλ'), on the one hand (μέν), the one from the slave woman has been born in accordance with the flesh, while on the other hand (δέ), the one from the free woman has been born through a promise (4:22–23).[31] Paul had previously proven that those who rely on faith are the true sons of Abraham (3:7). Only these belong to Christ and are Abraham's offspring. They are the heirs according to promise (3:29). Paul describing the son from the free woman as being born through a promise connects back to these established facts. In the Genesis narrative, the son from the free woman would be Isaac. He was born as the result of God's promise to open Sarah's womb (Gen 15:4; 17:16; 18:14; 21:1–2). The son of the slave woman would be Ishmael. Sarah had taken matters into her own hands to give Abraham an heir through her

---

29. As Levinsohn notes, the absence of a conjunction, "tell me," and the direct address "those who want to be under the law" support seeing a new subunit beginning at 4:21. The latter two features also give prominence to the question "Do you listen to the law?" ("Galatians," 323).

30. Similarly, DeSilva, *Galatians*, 392.

31. The μέν . . . δέ construction presents a counterpoint-point set that draws more attention to the point that the one from the free woman has been born through a promise (Runge, *Discourse Greek New Testament*, Gal 4:23).

slave Hagar. While Abraham had two sons, only Isaac and not Ishmael was God's promised heir for Abraham (Gen 17:18–19).[32]

Interestingly, Paul clarifies that he draws on these two women and their sons as an allegory. He explains (γάρ) that these women represent two covenants (δύο διαθῆκαι). On the one hand (μὲν), the one from Mount Sinai who brings people to birth into slavery is Hagar. Hagar represents Mount Sinai in Arabia.[33] She corresponds to the present Jerusalem, for (γάρ) she is enslaved along with her children. On the other hand (δὲ), the Jerusalem above, who is our mother, is free (4:24–26). Paul's allegorical interpretation appears to be that the narrative reveals principles concerning two covenants. The one associated with Hagar is an arrangement based on the flesh and perpetuates slavery. The other is based on promise and leads to freedom.[34] This depiction supports Paul's prior portrayal of living under the law as living in a state of slavery (4:3–5). He has also previously established the priority of God's promises to Abraham as a covenant (3:15–18). Paul makes explicit an underlying premise in his arguments in 3:7—4:7: the true children of Abraham come through inheriting God's promise to Abraham by faith and not through biological descent from Abraham.[35]

Back in 2:4, Paul had already contrasted the freedom we have in Christ Jesus with the slavery brought by the false brothers (linked with trying to impose circumcision as required by the law). Paul also depicted the Galatians' past situation under the law as a state of slavery (4:1–7). Submitting to doing what the law requires amounts to a return to slavery (4:8–11). In further support of his interpretation, Paul appeals to Isa 54:1: "For [γάρ] it is written: 'Rejoice, barren woman who is not giving birth; writhe and cry out, you who are not in labor, because [ὅτι] many more are the children of the desolate woman than of the woman who has a husband'" (4:28). Sarah is also called barren (Gen 11:30). She laughed (likely seen as closely related to shouting for joy) when she gave birth to Isaac (Gen 21:6–7). It is noteworthy as well that Isa 54:1 follows immediately after Isaiah describes the suffering servant of God who redeems many (Isa 52:13—53:12). Paul would have seen this passage as fulfilled by the death and resurrection of Jesus Christ.[36]

---

32. Similarly, Runge, *Galatians*, Gal 4:21–31.

33. The textual tradition is uncertain as to whether the conjunction δέ or γάρ should be read and whether Ἀγάρ should be omitted. On the whole, the evidence favors reading τὸ δὲ Ἀγάρ. See Moo, *Galatians*, s.vv. "Looking at the Present: Children of the Promise" (Gal 4:21–31), "Additional Notes."

34. Similarly, DeSilva, *Galatians*, 396.

35. Moo, *Galatians*, s.vv. "Looking at the Present: Children of Promise" (Gal 4:21–31).

36. Similarly, Moo, *Galatians*, s.vv. "Looking at the Present: Children of Promise" (Gal 4:21–31); DeSilva, *Galatians*, 401–2.

These connections apparently allowed Paul to apply Isa 54:1 to the law-free gentile mission. The fact that all nations would be blessed in Abraham (Gal 3:8 reflecting Gen 12:3 and 18:18) that the Scriptures foresaw has come to pass. Christ has redeemed them from the curse of the law so that the blessing of Abraham might come through Christ Jesus to the gentiles (3:13–14). It can indeed be said that many more are the children of the desolate woman than of the woman who has a husband.

Next, Paul shifts to the second person and addresses his audience directly as brothers and sisters: Now (δέ) you, brothers, are children of promise according to Isaac (4:28). Here, Paul applies the allegory directly to the Galatians. Like Isaac, they are the children God promised to Abraham. Contrary to expectations, the children of promise were not acknowledged as the true heirs.[37] Instead (ἀλλ'), just as formerly the one born according to the flesh persecuted (ἐδίωκεν) the one born according to the Spirit, thus also now (4:29).[38] Paul appears to be comparing how Ishmael persecuted Isaac[39] to his opponents persecuting those given new life by the Spirit in Galatia. Paul himself used to participate in persecuting God's churches (1:13, 23). Contrary to expectation, this persecution did not shake the position of the children of promise. Instead (ἀλλά), the ones born according to the flesh are thrown out. Paul supports this idea by citing the course of action Sarah urged Abraham to undertake in Gen 21:10 (which God affirmed that Abraham should follow in Gen 21:12). He asks rhetorically what the Scriptures say. Then he proceeds to answer himself: "Cast out the slave woman and her son, for the son of the slave woman will not inherit along with the son of the free woman" (4:30). This means that they know that the son of the slave woman will not inherit along with the son of the free woman. They are already sure of their inheritance (3:26–29; 4:4–7). Therefore (διό) Paul and his audience are not sons of the slave woman, but of the free woman (4:31).[40] This is the content of what Paul wants his audience to recognize by heeding his call to listen to the law.[41]

37. I am assuming that an implied premise that relates to the persecution described in 4:29 explains the adversative (ἀλλ'). Moo posits a similar elided premise (*Galatians*, s.vv. "Looking at the Present: Children of Promise" [Gal 4:21–31]).

38. Significantly, one born according to the Spirit seems to be used interchangeably with one born through promise (4:23) and children of promise (4:28). They are the antithesis of one born according to the flesh (4:23, 29). This is consistent with Paul's identification of the Spirit as the promised inheritance (3:13–14). It foreshadows Paul's discussion of living the Spirit's empowerment to rise above the power of the flesh (5:16–6:10).

39. It is unclear if Paul is appealing to Gen 21:9 only, where Sarah saw Ishmael playing or laughing during Isaac's weaning festivities.

40. Paul uses an inclusive "we."

41. Because the content of the call and the call itself are closely linked together, I chose to include both in the heading for this paragraph, which represents what I see as the main point.

GALATIANS 5:1—6:10

OUTLINE

II. First Round of Rebuke, Backed by Extended Support (1:6—2:21)

III. Second Round of Rebuke, Backed by Extended Support (3:1—4:7)

IV. Third Round of Rebuke (4:8–31)

V. **Extended Exhortation with Fourth Round of Rebuke Embedded (5:1—6:10)**

    A. **Stand Firm in Freedom, and Do Not Be Subject Again to Slavery (5:1-15)**

    B. **Walk in the Spirit, and You Will Not Carry Out the Desire of the Flesh (5:16-26)**

    C. **Let Us Work What Is Good for All, While We Have the Opportunity (6:1-10)**

V. EXTENDED EXHORTATION WITH FOURTH ROUND OF REBUKE EMBEDDED (5:1—6:10)

IT WAS RELATIVELY EASY to distinguish the letter opening (1:1-5), the first round of rebuke (1:6—2:21), and the second round of rebuke (3:1—4:7). If seeing 4:8-31 as a third round of rebuke was the hardest decision to make, seeing 5:1—6:10 as involving a fourth round of rebuke was a close second. Why is it so hard to classify this section? The quick shift from exhortation to warning and rebuke and then back to exhortation throws off attempts to neatly categorize it. First, a decisive shift away from rebuke to exhortation does not become sustained until 5:16. Second, after the exhortation in 5:1, Paul turns to warning (with implicit negative appraisal) in 5:2-4 and outright rebuke in

5:7–12. In the end, it seemed best to see (1) the warning in 5:2–4 (and the support of it in 5:5–6) as supporting the exhortation; and (2) the rebuke in 5:7–12 (and the support of it in 5:13–15) as on the same theme line. Appeal, warning, and rebuke thus coexist in this section of extended exhortation.

At the highest level of the discourse, I see four main points after the letter opening as:

1. I am astonished that you are so quickly turning away from the divine gospel brought to you by a divinely appointed servant of Christ.
2. O foolish Galatians, I want to learn from you whether you received the Spirit through doing what the law requires or through hearing accompanied by faith.
3. How can you return again to the weak and poor elements?
4. Stand firm in freedom, and do not be subject again to slavery!

Table 29 below provides an overview of the flow of 5:1—6:10 as a whole.

Table 29: Overview of the Flow of 5:1—6:10				
Connector	At	Connects	With	Function
None	5:1	5:1—6:10	1:6—4:31	Major break. Switches to exhortation (stand firm in freedom and do not return to slavery)
δέ	5:16	5:16–26	5:1–15	Exhortation (walk in the Spirit)
None	6:1	6:1–10	5:1–26	Minor break. Exhortation (work what is good for all)

A. Stand Firm in Freedom, and Do Not Be Subject Again to Slavery (5:1–15)

Table 30: The Flow of 5:1–15				
Connector	At	Connects	With	Function
None	5:1a	5:1—6:10	1:6—4:31	Major break. But uses lexical and conceptual repetition to summarize 1:6—4:31 to set the stage (for freedom Christ has set us free)
οὖν	5:1b	5:1b	5:1a	Infers (from 5:1a to stand firm in freedom and not return to slavery)
Closely related concept	5:2	5:2	1:6—5:1	Specific warning
δέ	5:3	5:3–6	5:2	Elaborates (warning and consequences)
Closely related concepts	5:4	5:4	5:3	Specific (two more consequences)
γάρ	5:5	5:5–6	5:1-4	Support (for warnings)
γάρ	5:6	5:6	5:5	Support (for waiting in way described)
Closely related concept	5:7a	5:7–15	1:6—5:6	Positive appraisal (of the past)
Closely related concept	5:7b	5:7b	1:6—5:7a	Rebuke
Closely related concept	5:8	5:8	1:6—5:7	Negative appraisal (of false gospel)
Analogy	5:9	5:9	1:6—5:8	Compares (and reinforces appraisal)
Closely related concept	5:10a	5:10a	1:6—5:9	Positive appraisal (of Galatians)
δέ	5:10b	5:10b	5:10a	Contrasts (with appraisal of opponents)

δέ	5:11a	5:11a	5:10b	Contrasts (with Paul's experience)
ἄρα	5:11b	5:11b	5:11a	Infers (negative result from 5:11a)
Closely related concept	5:12	5:12	5:7–11	Negative appraisal (wish opponents would castrate themselves)
γάρ	5:13a	5:13–15	5:7–11	Supports (warnings and appraisals)
μόνον	5:13b	5:13b	5:13a	Exception
ἀλλά	5:13c	5:13c	5:13b	Corrects (in contrast)
γάρ	5:14	5:14	5:13c	Supports (correct conduct)
δέ	5:15	5:15	5:14	Contrasts (bad conduct and result)

After effectively contrasting a life of slavery under the law and inheriting Abraham's blessing through faith in God's promise, Paul has prepared his audience well to hear and embrace his exhortations. How does Paul tie together his rebuke, exposition, and exhortations? Like in 4:8–9, Paul summarizes a big takeaway (likely for all of 1:6—4:31), using lexical and conceptual repetition. Indeed, "Christ set us free for freedom"[1] links to the already-established concepts of freedom, redemption, and slavery.[2] In 2:4, the freedom enjoyed through Christ was contrasted with the slavery brought by the false brothers (linked with trying to impose circumcision as required by the law). The Galatians used to be in a state of slavery under the law (4:1–7), and submitting to doing what the law requires would amount to a return to slavery (4:8–11). In contrast, Christ has redeemed them from the curse of the law so that the blessing of Abraham might come through Christ Jesus to the gentiles (3:13–14; see also 4:5). So, while the most immediate connection is to the conclusion of 4:21–31 (i.e., Paul and his audience are not sons of the slave woman, but of the free woman), the connections are broader throughout the letter. "Christ set us free for freedom" is thus an effective

---

1. Paul uses an inclusive "us." Note that there are some textual variants that apparently arise from the sequence Τῇ ἐλευθερίᾳ ... ἠλευθέρωσεν being unexpected. See Moo, *Galatians*, s.vv. "Justified by Faith and Not by the Law" (Gal 5:1–6), "Additional Notes."

2. The lexical words that convey the concepts of "freedom," "redemption," and "slavery" belong under domain 37, "Control, Rule," L&N 1:471–88. ἐλευθερία (2:4; 5:1, 13 [2x]), ἐλεύθερος (4:22, 23, 26, 30, 31), ἐλευθερόω (5:1), and ἐξαγοράζω (3:13; 4:5) belong under "Release, Set Free" (37.127–37.138). δουλόω (4:3), καταδουλόω (2:4), δουλεύω (4:8, 9, 25), δουλεία (4:24; 5:1), and δοῦλος belong under "Control, Restrain" (37.1–37.32). Note that I would include the occurrences in 4:1, 7 only for δοῦλος as the occurrences in 1:10 and 3:28 function differently.

summary of the letter so far. At the same time, this summary serves as the ground for the inferred obligation to heed Paul's exhortation that follows.[3]

Since this is what Christ has done, therefore (οὖν), stand firm, and do not be subject again to a yoke of slavery. This is the main point of 5:1–15 and of the whole letter so far. At this point, one might expect Paul to continue in his exhortations. Nevertheless, his extended appeal is postponed again until 5:16.

Why would Paul choose to interrupt his appeal yet again? The abrupt change in 5:2 without any connecting words signals another shift. The exhortations of v. 1 are supported by 5:2–6. Both "behold" and "I, Paul, say to you" function to draw extra attention to what follows: If they receive circumcision, Christ will not profit them at all.[4] Paul effectively highlights his negative evaluation of this potential scenario. It seems that Paul saw the need to elaborate on the dangers of circumcision.

This is Paul's first explicit mention of circumcision since his description of his visit to Jerusalem in 2:3 (where even Titus was not compelled to be circumcised). The depth of the association of circumcision with the Jewish law can be seen in Gal 2:7–9, for example, where Jews and gentiles can be referred to as circumcised and uncircumcised. As the sign of God's covenant with Abraham and his physical descendants, the many references to works of the law and being under the law throughout the letter undoubtedly evoked circumcision in Paul's audience's mind. If the audience accepts circumcision, they would, in effect, be taking on the keeping of the Jewish law.[5] Paul warns that the cost is to lose any benefit from Christ's redemption of them.

Paul also warns about the flip side. Just as he warned in v. 2 about an unimaginable loss, he testified again to every man who receives circumcision that he is a debtor to do the whole law (5:3).[6] You not only get no benefit, but you incur an impossible debt![7] This recalls Paul's earlier warnings from Scripture that "cursed is everyone who does not remain in all the

---

3. See Schreiner, *Galatians*, 307. Besides the conceptual connections to freedom, redemption, and slavery already pointed out above, I do not think "Christ set us free for freedom" can be explained adequately as a summary of 4:21–31 alone because Christ's work is assumed rather than developed in that unit.

4. Runge, *Galatians*, Gal 5:1–15.

5. Runge, *Galatians*, Gal 5:1–15.

6. Runge, *Galatians*, Gal 5:1–15.

7. DeSilva notes Paul's clever wordplay: Christ will not "benefit" or "oblige" (ὠφελήσει [5:2]) those who, by being circumcised, make themselves "debtors" or "people obligated to" (ὀφειλέτης) keep the whole law (5:3) (*Galatians*, 417).

things written in the book of the law to do them" (3:10) and "the one who does these things shall live by them" (3:12).

Paul continues by highlighting closely related consequences:[8] whoever among you is trying to be justified by the law is cut off (κατηργήθητε) from Christ.[9] You have fallen from grace (5:4). We already know from Gal 3:11 that no one is justified before God by means of the law. While the law could not nullify (καταργῆσαι) the promise (3:17), the association of Paul's audience with Christ would effectively be nullified (κατηργήθητε).[10] This would represent a reversal of their union with Christ (depicted previously as being baptized into Christ, having put on Christ, being one in Christ Jesus, and belonging to Christ in 3:27–29). The grace they have fallen away from is the grace of Christ to which God has called them (1:6). When God's grace is rejected, Christ would have died in vain (2:21).

The reason (γάρ) for warning against receiving circumcision and taking on the obligation of doing the whole law is that righteousness comes by a different path: Paul and his audience are waiting for the hope of righteousness through the Spirit by faith (5:5).[11] This is because (γάρ) in Christ Jesus neither circumcision nor uncircumcision has any force, but rather (ἀλλά) faith working through love is what has force (5:6). So far, our interpretation of "justify" (δικαιόω) and "righteousness" (δικαιοσύνη) has assumed that they involve God declaring a status of being righteous. This assumption is supported by Paul's fundamental appeal to Abraham being considered righteous before God when he believed God's promise (3:6). Paul and his audience have already been declared righteous through faith in Christ (2:16; 3:24). They have received the promised Spirit (3:14; 4:6). Nevertheless, while they received the Spirit through faith (3:2), they were in danger of being convinced to seek completion in the flesh (3:3). So, it seems the Galatians must continue as they began (through the Spirit by faith). Otherwise, Paul would not be so concerned that they were in danger of being cut off from Christ and falling from grace.[12] The Galatians must continue to await a future hoped-for righteousness through the Spirit by faith. This hoped-for righteousness appears to be God's final verdict on the last day.[13]

Through the Spirit by faith, a transformation is also in process. This appears to be what Paul referred to as: (1) Christ living in him (which

---

8. Runge, *Galatians*, Gal 5:1–15.
9. Moo, *Galatians*, s.vv. "Justified by Faith and Not by the Law" (Gal 5:1–6).
10. Bruce, *Galatians*, 231.
11. Paul uses an inclusive "we."
12. Moo, *Galatians*, s.vv. "Justified by Faith and Not by the Law" (Gal 5:1–6).
13. Schreiner, *Galatians*, 316.

involves him living by faith in Christ [2:20]) and (2) Christ being formed in the Galatians (4:19). Paul seems to expect the Galatians not only to begin in the Spirit, but also to continue to complete their journey in the Spirit (not in the flesh through the law [3:3]). Paul likely already has in mind believers being transformed into Spirit-led people who do what pleases God, which he will develop further in 5:16—6:10. It is by living Spirit led and Spirit transformed that they can confidently wait for and look forward to the ultimate vindication of their righteous status before God.[14]

The reason (γὰρ) they can have this confident hope is two-fold: Negatively, in Christ Jesus, neither circumcision nor uncircumcision has any force. Positively, by contrast, faith working through love has force (5:6). Paul has already established that just like everyone else, even Jewish Christians must be justified through faith in Christ and not through the works of the law (2:16). Jews and Greeks alike are sons of God through faith in Christ Jesus (3:26-29). So, the state of being circumcised or being uncircumcised or what they represent (i.e., keeping the law) has no relevance. Being a Jew and thus being circumcised and keeping the law contributes nothing whatsoever to being found righteous before God. By first putting aside what does not matter, what truly matters comes to the forefront by contrast. Paul says that this is faith working through love. Those who are in Christ live through the Spirit by faith. This faith also works powerfully through love. Later in Gal 5:22, love will also be characterized as a fruit of the Spirit's work in their lives. Faith and the Spirit are thus sufficient not only to gain entry into God's family, but also for living lives pleasing to God, all the way till God's final judgment on the last day.[15]

Next, Paul affirms that the Galatians started well and returns to discrediting his opponents: he uses race imagery. You were running well. Who hindered you so that you did not obey the truth? (5:7). As in 3:1-6, Paul is uninterested in the perpetrators' identity, quickly moving on without answering this question. Paul's concern was that the truth of the gospel might remain with gentile Christians like his Galatian audience (2:5). Like when he confronted Cephas for not being straightforward about the truth of the gospel (2:14), he intervenes here as well. The rhetorical question follows the pattern of rebuke established previously: if no one could legitimately turn the Galatians away from obeying the truth, then hindering them from proceeding in their existing course should not happen.[16]

---

14. Moo, *Galatians*, s.vv. "Justified by Faith and Not by the Law" (Gal 5:1-6).

15. Similarly, Moo, *Galatians*, s.vv. "Justified by Faith and Not by the Law" (Gal 5:1-6).

16. Similarly, DeSilva, *Galatians*, 432-33.

Recalling his opening allegation ("I am astonished that you are so quickly turning away from the one who called you" [1:6]), Paul reiterates that this persuasion is not from the one who called you (5:8). Paul reinforces his point with some proverbial wisdom: a little yeast leavens the whole lump (5:9). This is a practical appeal to everyday experience in baking bread.[17] It was frequently used figuratively in the New Testament and other ancient writings to depict evil's penetrating and corrupting influence.[18] So, Paul paints the perpetrators in full color as involved in spreading evil.

Despite his concerns, Paul reaffirms his belief that they will agree with him: I myself am persuaded in the Lord concerning you that you will think no other way (5:10). Paul seems to engage in a wordplay with the same verb used in vv. 7 and 10 and its cognate noun in v. 8: "Who has hindered you from being persuaded to follow [πείθεσθαι] the truth?" (5:7). "Such persuasion [πεισμονὴ] is not from God" (5:8). "I myself am persuaded [πέποιθα] about you" (5:10).[19] The overall message would be that Paul is convinced that the rival teachers will not convince the Galatians. This is consistent with Paul's use of inclusive language to move the Galatians to agree with him (e.g., 3:13–14, 23–25; 4:3–6, 26, 31; 5:1, 5).[20] It is also consistent with his assessment that they were running well (5:6) and his prior appeal to their lived experience of believing the gospel and receiving the Spirit (3:1–6). Paul is convinced they received the gospel and are indeed his brothers and sisters in Christ. Hence, he can be confident they will ultimately agree with him against the false teachers.[21] In addition (δὲ), Paul is equally confident that the one confusing (ὁ ταράσσων) them will bear his judgment, whoever he is (5:10). This recalls "those who are confusing [οἱ ταράσσοντες] you and who want to distort the gospel of Christ" (1:7). This can apply to anyone. Even in the unlikelihood that it was Paul or an angel from heaven (1:8), any such person was cursed (1:8–9).

Paul adds: "Moreover [δέ], as for me, brothers and sisters, if I still preach circumcision, why am I still persecuted [διώκομαι]?" (5:11). It is unclear when Paul might or might not have preached circumcision.[22] It is clear, however, that the rhetorical question assumes that Paul was still being persecuted. The hypothetical scenario of Paul still preaching circumcision is false. The point is that this persecution proves that he was not still advocating

17. DeSilva, *Galatians*, 434.
18. Longenecker, *Galatians*, 231.
19. Moo, *Galatians*, s.vv. "Resisting the Agitators" (Gal 5:7–12).
20. See table 4, "First-Person Plural References."
21. Similarly, Bruce, *Galatians*, 235.
22. Schreiner, *Galatians*, 326–27.

circumcision. Before he was converted, Paul himself persecuted (ἐδίωκον) the church beyond measure and tried to destroy it in his zeal to uphold his inherited Jewish traditions (1:13–14). This would have included a belief that God only accepted circumcised people who followed the Jewish law.[23]

If Paul were still to advocate circumcision, then the stumbling block of the cross would be nullified (5:11). What does this stumbling block involve? The cross evokes Christ's crucifixion, and advocating circumcision somehow nullifies this. Galatians 3:1 comes to mind where Paul rebukes the Galatians for not perceiving the significance of Christ crucified. There Paul reminded the Galatians that they received the Spirit through "hearing of faith" rather than "works of the law." If these things are related, the stumbling block of the cross starts with a crucified Messiah, who died under the curse of God's law (3:13). Because no one can be justified by the works of the law, even Jewish Christians must be justified through faith in Christ and not through the works of the law (2:16). As established in Gal 3:7—4:7, only those who rely on faith are Abraham's true heirs. More specifically, Gal 3:15—4:7 proved that inheritance depends not on law but on God's promise. The heart of the issue seems to be gentiles being accepted into God's family on equal terms with Jews through faith in the crucified Messiah, without requiring circumcision and keeping of the Jewish law.[24] Paul was intimately acquainted with the stumbling block of the cross because he used to persecute the church and was now proclaiming the faith that he was formerly trying to destroy (1:23). Paul goes so far as to conclude with a wish that those troubling the Galatians go beyond circumcision and even castrate themselves (5:12).[25] This wish confirms that circumcision is at the center of contention not only in 5:11–12, but also likely in 5:7–12 and the rest of the letter.

Next, Paul offers the reasons (γὰρ) for his expressions of concern, discrediting of his opponents, and even his blunt wish.[26] This pattern recalls his presentation of supporting reasons after similar expressions of astonishment, undermining the other gospel, and curse pronouncement in 1:6–9. He is reacting so strongly because his Galatian brothers and sisters were called to freedom (5:13, which recalls "Christ set us free for freedom" in 5:1). In

---

23. Nicolle, "Conditionals in Galatians," 105–6.

24. Similarly, DeSilva, *Galatians*, 439–40.

25. DeSilva notes that the verb ἀποκόπτω may recall the ruling in Deut 23:2 that excludes a man whose male genitalia "has been cut off" from entering the assembly of the Lord. Paul may be wishing that his opponents would make themselves unfit for the congregation of Israel as a fitting judgment for threatening the place of the gentile Galatians in Christ's church by trying to get them to receive circumcision (*Galatians*, 440–41).

26. Runge, *Galatians*, Gal 5:1–15.

5:1, Paul moved from this premise to the conclusion that the Galatians must not be subject again to a yoke of slavery, such as circumcision and the Jewish law. Now, Paul builds on the same premise to provide positive instruction on how to live in that freedom. The only qualification (μόνον) is that this freedom is not an opportunity for the flesh (ἀφορμὴν τῇ σαρκί).[27] Instead (ἀλλὰ), the intent is to serve (δουλεύετε) one another through love (5:13). Put another way, the freedom for which Christ set them free is a freedom to serve others through love. It was never intended to become an opportunity to indulge the desires of fallen human beings.[28] True freedom paradoxically manifests itself as a new form of slavery (δουλεύετε).[29] Unlike the weak and poor elements to which they would not want to be enslaved again (4:8–9), they would want to embrace serving one another through love. The noun "love" (ἀγάπη) occurs in 5:13 and 5:22. Its cognate verb ἀγαπάω occurs in 5:14. However, the concept is not restricted to these verses. Conceptually, love takes center stage for the whole of 5:13—6:10. The word "one another" (ἀλλήλων) is also sprinkled throughout (5:13, 15 [2x], 17, 26 [2x]; 6:2), while occurring nowhere else in the letter. It highlights the reciprocal concern that love has for others.[30]

It is fitting for Christian freedom to express itself this way because (γὰρ) such loving service to others fulfills the whole law: The whole law is fulfilled in one commandment, namely, "You shall love your neighbor as [you love] yourself" (5:14). However, did Paul not just finish warning the Galatians not to receive circumcision because they would become obligated to keep the whole law (5:3)? How can he so quickly turn around to call on the same audience to do something that fulfills the whole law? He even cites Lev 19:18.[31]

---

27. DeSilva notes that ἀφορμή may evoke the image of a base of operations for a military campaign. Paul may have this in mind as he goes on to depict the Spirit and the flesh at war with each other (5:16–17). If this is the case, then Paul is warning against giving the flesh a base from which to attack by misusing Christian freedom (*Galatians*, 446).

28. Moo has a good discussion of how σάρξ refers variously to the soft tissues of the human body, the human body as a whole, human beings as a whole, or the general condition of being human. Sometimes the human condition is without regard for sin (though often with a hint of limitation). Sometimes (as in Gal 5:13–25) the human condition fully limited by sin is in view (*Galatians*, s.vv. "The Basic Pattern of the New Life: Serving One Another in Love" [Gal 5:13–15]).

29. Schreiner, *Galatians*, 333–34.

30. Similarly, Moo, *Galatians*, s.vv. "The Basic Pattern of the New Life: Serving One Another in Love" (Gal 5:13–15).

31. Schreiner, *Galatians*, 334.

It may help to remember Paul's previous articulation about the priority of faith in saying that faith working through love has force (5:6). Revisiting Paul's statements in Gal 2:19–21 (filling in some blanks about what is involved in Christ's death on the cross to bring redemption from 3:1—4:7) and reconstructing its logic also may shed some light. Through their union with Christ by faith, Paul (and all believers with him) are considered crucified together with Christ. The law cursed Christ and condemned him to death for the sins of those united with him. They are considered to have died together with Christ on the cross. Together with Christ, they are considered dead to the law and are no longer obligated to it. They (in the sense of their human condition limited by sin) no longer live. Instead, Christ lives in them through the Spirit. It is a transformed human life lived by faith in the Son of God who loved them and gave himself for them (2:19–21). The purpose is that they can live for God. Christ redeeming them (from being obligated to the law) and giving them the Spirit through faith results in the true fulfillment of the law. This fulfillment happens when Christians love others with a love possible only for those who, through the Spirit by faith, wait for the future hoped-for righteousness (5:5).[32] Practically, what does this fulfillment involve? We will find out in 5:16—6:10 what Paul has in mind as applied to the Galatians.

Meanwhile, Paul adds a contrasting scenario (δὲ) to the loving service he just prescribed for how Christians should interact with one another.[33] Those who were trying to follow the law were apparently embroiled in divisions and infighting:[34] But if you bite and devour one another, beware lest you be consumed by one another (5:15). Biting (δάκνω), devouring (κατεσθίω), and "consuming" (ἀναλίσκω) together paint a picture of animals tearing into one another, with each action escalating the situation.[35]

---

32. Similarly, Moo, *Galatians*, s.vv. "The Basic Pattern of the New Life: Serving One Another in Love" (Gal 5:13–15).

33. DeSilva, *Galatians*, 451.

34. Runge, *Galatians*, Gal 5:1–15.

35. DeSilva, *Galatians*, 451.

B. Walk in the Spirit, and You Will Not Carry Out the Desire of the Flesh (5:16–26)

Table 31: The Flow of 5:16–26				
Connector	At	Connects	With	Function
δέ	5:16a	5:16–26	5:1–15	Elaborates (resumes exhortations in 5:1)
καὶ	5:16b	5:16b	5:16a	Associated (result)
γὰρ	5:17a	5:17a–24	5:16	Supports (exhortation and associated result in 5:16a–b)
δὲ	5:17b	5:17b	5:17a	Contrasts (the flesh's and the Spirit's desires against each other)
γὰρ	5:17c	5:17c–24	5:17a–b	Supports (contrast)
ἵνα	5:17d	5:17d	5:17c	Result (not able to do what you desire)
δὲ	5:18	5:18	5:16–17	Contrasts (stalemate with scenario of not under law when led by the Spirit)
δέ	5:19	5:19–21a	5:16–18	Elaborates (on what the flesh does)
Relative clause	5:21b	5:21b	5:19–21a	Negative appraisal (warns of not inheriting the kingdom of God)
δὲ	5:22	5:22–23a	5:16–21	Contrasts (what the Spirit does)
Demonstrative	5:23b	5:23b	5:22–23a	Positive appraisal (no law against)
δὲ	5:24	5:24	5:16–23	Elaborates (on state of those who belong to Christ)
Closely related concept	5:25	5:25	5:16–24	Resumes exhortation (call based on true scenario)
Closely related concept	5:26	5:26	5:16–25	Contrasts (warns against incorrect conduct and destructive results)

Paul launches into his prescribed antidote with the obviously flesh-driven behavior warned against in 5:15 serving as the immediate foil. The foundation is walking in step with the Spirit (5:16–26). If they persevere in working what is good in the Spirit by faith, they will reap eternal life at the final judgment (6:1–10).

The imperative in 5:16 signals a shift back to appeal. This time Paul fully develops the positive appeal he started with the last imperative at 5:1 (but interrupted with more rebuke): walk by the Spirit, and you will not carry out the desire (ἐπιθυμίαν) of the flesh. This is the main point of 5:16–26 and a coordinated second main point for 5:1—6:10. How did I make this determination? Λέγω δέ (Moreover, I say) simultaneously highlights this prescription and coordinates this section to the last higher-level exhortation at 5:1.[36] Paul also prepared the way by already qualifying freedom as not an opportunity for the flesh (5:13) and offering love as an alternative to the law (5:13–14). However, he does not directly expound on how love is related to his next point. Where does this love come from? How is it related to the Spirit? We must hold on to our question and read on for now.

Instead of continuing to explain, Paul issues an exhortation to walk by the Spirit (5:16) in coordination with his previous appeal to stand firm and not be subject to a yoke of slavery (5:1). Why would Paul offer walking by the Spirit as the proper alternative to obeying the law? How can Paul assure the Galatians that they will not carry out the desire of the flesh?[37] What do we know so far about the Spirit that might explain why walking by the Spirit can succeed where the law failed? This is the Spirit God gave the Galatians when they believed in the crucified Christ (3:2–5). This Spirit also grants them an intimate relationship with God as their Father (4:6–7). Walking by the Spirit refers to the same underlying reality as Christ living in them. It also involves living by faith in the Son of God who loved them and gave himself for them (2:20). It is not too surprising, then, that by walking by the Spirit in this way, the Galatians would simultaneously stand firm in freedom (5:1) and not allow the flesh to misuse their freedom (5:13).[38]

Next, Paul supports (γάρ) his call to walk by the Spirit: "For the flesh desires [ἐπιθυμεῖ] against the Spirit, and the Spirit desires against the flesh." He further explains (γάρ):[39] "For these are opposed to one another, so that you cannot do what you desire" (5:17). In other words, the flesh and the

---

36. Similarly, Runge, *Galatians*, Gal 5:16–26.

37. The doubly negated aorist subjunctive second-person plural verb construction here (οὐ μὴ τελέσητε) might also be read as a prohibition, "and do not carry out the desire of the flesh." Evidence of usage elsewhere seems to favor seeing it as an emphatic statement about future outcomes. See Keener, *Galatians*, s.vv. "Following the Spirit's Steps" (Gal 5:16–25); DeSilva, *Galatians*, 454.

38. Similarly, DeSilva, *Galatians*, 452–53.

39. It is uncertain whether γάρ or δέ should be read. The difference is small in this case: either explaining the warring desires of the flesh and the Spirit as due to their fundamental opposition to each other or elaborating further on this characteristic. See Moo, *Galatians*, s.vv. "Implementing the New Life: Walking by the Spirit" (Gal 5:16–24), "Additional Notes."

Spirit are diametrically opposed. What each one desires is contrary to the other. The result is not being able to do what you desire (θέλητε, whether it matches what the Spirit or the flesh desires). The Galatians must choose to walk by the Spirit to break this stalemate and experience being led by the Spirit.[40] Moreover (δέ), Paul reminds them that "if you are led by the Spirit, you are not under the law" (5:18). Paul had previously closely related the opposition between hearing of faith and works of the law (3:2) with beginning in the Spirit and finishing in the flesh (3:3). The result is that the flesh is linked with works of the law and the Spirit with living by faith.[41] In 5:18, the Spirit and the law are directly opposed. This opposition was also implied throughout 3:7—4:7 as only those who believe in Christ are Abraham's true heirs, who inherit the promised Spirit. We know that Abraham's true sons and heirs are no longer slaves under the law (4:1–7).

Greek, Hellenistic, and Roman ethical literature often had lists of vices and virtues. Unsurprisingly, Paul puts together a list of vices to illustrate the works associated with the flesh. Paul may also have intentionally highlighted vices that involve an absence or a perversion of love for others: "Now [δέ] the works of the flesh are evident. They are sexual immorality, impurity, sensuality, idolatry, sorcery, enmities, strife, jealousy, bursts of rage, contentiousness, dissensions, factions, envy, drunkenness, carousing, and things like these" (5:19–21).[42] With the words "things like these," we know this is a representative rather than a comprehensive list.[43] The contrasted alternative (headed by love) is this: "But [δέ] the fruit associated with the Spirit is love, joy, peace, patience, kindness, goodness, faithfulness,[44] gentleness, and self-control" (5:22–23). The vastly different results of living in accordance with the desires of the flesh versus walking in line with the Spirit's desires are obvious.[45] Their very different effects on community relationships are also evident.[46]

The difference in outcomes for those whose lives exhibit the vice list versus the virtue list is equally stark. Concerning the vice list, Paul solemnly tells the Galatians in advance, just as he had warned them before, that those

---

40. Similarly, Runge, *Galatians*, Gal 5:16–26.

41. Runge, *Galatians*, Gal 5:16–26.

42. Some witnesses add "adultery" before "sexual immorality," and some add "murders" after "envy." These were likely assimilated to other vice lists (e.g., Matt 15:19 and Rom 1:29 respectively).

43. DeSilva, *Galatians*, 458–59.

44. πίστις could potentially mean faith here too. However, in a virtue list, nestled between "goodness" and "gentleness," it more likely means "faithfulness."

45. DeSilva, *Galatians*, 458.

46. Moo, *Galatians*, s.vv. "Implementing the New Life: Walking by the Spirit" (Gal 5:16–24).

who practice these things will not inherit the kingdom of God (5:21).[47] By commenting on his current forewarning and mentioning his prior warning, Paul put tremendous stress on his warning.[48]

For people whose lives exhibit the virtue list, Paul declares that there is no law against such things (5:23). Paul's declaration may recall a statement by Aristotle. Speaking about people who exhibited uncommon moral excellence, Aristotle said that "against such people as these there is no law." Paul and Aristotle may share a similar notion that people with well-developed virtues are the type of people a fair and virtuous body of laws aims to cultivate. By embodying these virtues, they invariably remain on the right side of the law.[49] In addition, we should not overlook the fact that Paul finally answered the question about where the love that fulfills the law comes from: It is the fruit of the Spirit (5:22). So, walking by the Spirit will inevitably involve loving your neighbor as you love yourself.

Furthermore (δὲ), those who belong to Christ Jesus have crucified the flesh with its passions and desires (5:24).[50] This assertion helps explain how Paul can assure the Galatians that they will not carry out the desire of the flesh by heeding his call to walk by the Spirit. Revisiting Paul's statements in Gal 2:19-21 may again provide further insight.[51] Through their union with Christ by faith, Paul (and all believers with him) are considered crucified together with Christ. The law cursed Christ and condemned him to death for the sins of those united with him (3:13). They are considered to have died together with Christ on the cross. Together with Christ, they are considered dead to the flesh and its passion and desires. They (in the sense of their human condition limited by sin) no longer live. Instead, Christ lives in them through the Spirit. It is a transformed human life lived by faith in the Son of God who loved them and gave himself for them (2:19-21).

To recap, why does Paul call on the Galatians to walk in the Spirit and promise that doing so they will not carry out the desire of the flesh (5:16)? First, the Spirit and the flesh desire opposite things, and they would want to be led by the Spirit (5:17-18). Second, they are no longer under the law (5:18-23). Third, they are considered dead to the flesh and its passions and desires (5:24). Paul appeals to the life the Spirit has already given them. They had

---

47. This exclusion from the eschatological inheritance is also clearly taught in 1 Cor 6:9-10 and Eph 5:5 (Schreiner, *Galatians*, 348).

48. DeSilva, *Galatians*, 463.

49. DeSilva, *Galatians*, 468-69.

50. "Jesus" in "those who belong to Christ Jesus" is uncertain, but the manuscript evidence favors its inclusion.

51. Similarly, Schreiner, *Galatians*, 351.

begun in the Spirit (3:3) and received the promised Spirit through faith (3:14). The Spirit produces the kind of fruit that is opposed to the flesh (5:19–23).

Paul shifts from addressing his audience in the second person to the inclusive first-person plural. He includes himself with his audience in these appeals and effectively softens his tone:[52] "If we live in the Spirit" (which is true), then "let us also walk in step with the Spirit" (5:25).[53] Paul's words in 5:16 and 5:25 recall each other and reinforce his appeal for the Galatians to stay in step with the Spirit.[54]

Before transitioning to the next section, Paul presents a contrasting scenario right next to his positive appeal to walk in step with the Spirit: Let us not become conceited, provoking one another, envying one another (5:26). This is similar to how he called the Galatians to loving service while warning them against biting and devouring one another, lest they be consumed by one another (5:15).[55] This repeated call shows that infighting was a problem among the Galatians. With this insight in mind, many items in the vice list also stand out in a new light as related to hostility and strife. ἔχθραι (enmities), ἔρις (strife), ἐριθεῖαι (contentiousness), and διχοστασίαι (dissensions) all fall within semantic domain 39, "Hostility, Strife."[56] αἱρέσεις (factions) likewise complements this picture with division of people into opposing groups.[57] θυμοί (bursts of rage) would seem to be frequently associated with hostility and strife as well. With communities rife with hostility and strife, it is no wonder that Paul calls them not to provoke one another (5:26) or devour one another (5:15). Likewise, the exhortation against envying (φθονοῦντες) one another (5:26) recalls envy (φθόνοι) and jealousy (ζῆλος) in the vice list.[58]

---

52. Runge, *Galatians*, Gal 5:16–26.

53. Nicolle, "Conditionals in Galatians," 107–8.

54. Schreiner, *Galatians*, 356–57. The verb στοιχέω may also contrast with στοιχεῖα in 4:3, 9. The idea may be to contrast keeping in step with the Spirit with their former enslavement to these weak and poor elements.

55. DeSilva, *Galatians*, 473.

56. L&N 1:491–501. Alternatively, ἐριθεῖαι may mean "selfish ambition," which may still be related (involving a feeling of resentfulness based upon jealousy and implying rivalry [domain 88.167, "ἐριθεῖαα, ας," L&N 1:760]).

57. Domain 63.27, "αἵρεσιςς, εως," L&N 1:615.

58. As Yoon notes, φθονοῦντες (envying) links to φθόνοι (envy) in 5:2 (*Discourse Analysis of Galatians*, 159). I would add ζῆλος (88.162) because it is very closely related to φθόνος (88.160) and φθονέω (88.161) within the same sub-domain (88.160–88.166, "Envy, Jealousy," L&N 1:759–60).

C. Let Us Work What Is Good for All, While We Have the Opportunity (6:1–10)

Table 32: The Flow of 6:1–10				
Connector	At	Connects	With	Function
None	6:1	6:1–10	5:16–26	Switches to specific exhortation, but has lexical and conceptual repetition to tie to 5:16–26
Analogy	6:2a	6:2a	6:1	Comparison (reinforces exhortation)
καὶ	6:2b	6:2b	6:2a	Associated (result)
γὰρ	6:3	6:3	6:1–2	Supports (exhortation with warning against improper self-assessment)
δὲ	6:4a	6:4–5	6:3	Contrasts (with exhortation to proper self-assessment)
καὶ (2x)	6:4b–c	6:4b–c	6:4a	Associated (results)
γὰρ	6:5	6:5	6:4	Supports (proper self-assessment)
δὲ	6:6	6:6	6:1–5	Distinct specific exhortation
Closely related concept	6:7a	6:7–10	5:1—6:6	Warning
γὰρ	6:7b	6:7b–8	6:7a	Supports (warning)
ὅτι	6:8a	6:8	6:7b	Reason
δὲ	6:8b	6:8b	6:8a	Contrasts (two scenarios)
δὲ	6:9a	6:9	5:1—6:8	Elaborates (summarizing exhortation)
γὰρ	6:9b	6:9b	6:9a	Supports (summarizing exhortation)
Ἄρα οὖν	6:10	6:10	5:1—6:9	Infers (climactic exhortation)

How does 6:1–10 relate to 5:16–26? Upon closer examination, it seems that after the general exhortations in 5:16–26, Paul gets specific in 6:1–10. He starts by redirecting his audience's attention by addressing them directly as "brothers and sisters." He also switches from the first-person plural back to the second-person plural: "Brothers and sisters, if anyone is overtaken in any trespass, you, who are spiritual, should restore such a one in a spirit of gentleness."⁵⁹ The scenario matches the situation in Galatia and the earlier situation with Cephas in Antioch. In both cases, believers were overtaken by sinful behavior (when they should have known better). Someone had to intervene to set them back on course.⁶⁰ The spiritual person was Paul in those cases. With those who are spiritual (οἱ πνευματικοί), Paul seems to connect back to his call to walk in step with the Spirit in 5:16–26. Those who are walking by the Spirit (5:16), are led by the Spirit (5:18), and are keeping in step with the Spirit (5:25) are to restore those who have gone astray. A spirit of gentleness (πνεύματι πραΰτητος) also connects back to gentleness (πραΰτης) as the fruit of the Spirit (5:23).⁶¹

Going one step further, I think this is a specific appeal targeted at the infighting Paul urged against previously. There were likely different degrees of receptivity or opposition to the teaching of the false teachers. Amid theological controversy, it is easy to imagine different factions among the Galatians metaphorically biting and devouring one another (5:15). Those who thought they knew better than their opponents could easily become conceited. Mutual provocation and mutual envy among the different groups could quickly run rampant (5:26). These behaviors would patently fall under the works of the flesh Paul outlined in 5:19–23. By outlining the fruit of the Spirit and highlighting what it looks like to be led by the Spirit, Paul guides the Galatians on what Spirit-led intervention looks like.⁶² This restoration process is also tempered by looking carefully at themselves lest they fall into temptation (6:1).

In any case, restoring any who have fallen back into works of the flesh is a specific example of love at work. The broader principle of bearing one another's burdens (6:2) is a general manifestation of serving one another through love. Slaves typically bear someone else's burdens. When you voluntarily bear one another's burdens, you practically demonstrate serving one another through love as slaves (5:13). Indeed, in this manner you will fulfill the law associated with Christ (6:2).⁶³ This links back to Paul's earlier claim that the whole law is fulfilled in one commandment, namely, "You shall love your neighbor as [you love] yourself" (5:14). Taking up a neighbor's burdens

---

59. Besides the direct address and the shift from first to second person, there is also no conjunction. These all support the start of a new paragraph at 6:1. See also Levinsohn, *Discourse Features*, appendix 17.3.

60. Runge, *Galatians*, Gal 6:1–10.

61. Schreiner, *Galatians*, 357–58.

62. Similarly, Runge, *Galatians*, Gal 6:1–10.

63. It is uncertain whether the future "you will fulfill" or imperative "fulfill" should be read. The evidence favors the future. See Moo, *Galatians*, s.vv. "Some Specific Parameters of the New Life" (Gal 5:25—6:6), "Additional Notes."

as one's own fulfills the command to love your neighbor as yourself. Within the context of Galatians, the law of Christ refers to serving one another through love as slaves and fulfilling the whole law in the commandment to love your neighbor as yourself (5:13–14). This would be in line with Jesus's teachings, with love for God and love for neighbor as the two most important commandments (Matt 22:39; Mark 12:31; Luke 10:27). In addition, it may point to Christ himself, who loved them and gave himself for them (Gal 2:20), as the paradigm of this love. As Christ is formed in them (2:20; 4:19) by the work of the Spirit, they lovingly serve more and more like Christ.[64] This would be consistent with Jesus's new commandment to his disciples to love one another as he has loved them (John 13:34–35; 15:12–17).

In Gal 6:3–5, Paul supports both his specific and general call to serve one another through love from vv. 1–2: "For [γὰρ] if anyone thinks himself to be something,[65] when he is nothing, he is deceiving himself. Moreover [δὲ], each one should examine his own work, and then he will have something to boast about relating to himself only, and not relating to another. For [γὰρ] each one will bear his own load." While one could see that a proud person might be unwilling to bear others' burdens, it is harder to link self-deception and the need to examine one's own work. However, these things match well with the need to rightly assess that one belongs in the category of those who are spiritual at any given point and to look carefully at oneself to avoid also falling into temptation (6:1). Bearing one another's burdens in v. 2 is then used as an analogy to support the specific appeal to restore any brothers or sisters who have strayed.[66] Verses 3–4 spell out the proper evaluation of oneself needed to undertake this restoration. This is consistent with Jesus's admonition first to take out the log in your own eye, and then you will see clearly to take the speck out of your brother's or sister's eye (Mat 7:5). At the same time, the stress on the need to assess oneself and examine one's own work properly begins to make clear that each person must still take responsibility for himself or herself.[67] In addition, each should be able to boast about their own work (the result of faith working through love and of the Spirit's leading in 5:1–26) rather than in someone else's at the final judgment.[68] Then, the same analogy of burden

---

64. Similarly, DeSilva, *Galatians*, 483–85.

65. In 2:2, 6, the verb δοκέω is used to refer to being esteemed by others to be important. Here it means to think oneself to be important.

66. Similarly, Lightfoot, *Galatians*, 216.

67. Runge, *Galatians*, Gal 6:1–10.

68. Schreiner, *Galatians*, 361–62.

bearing is applied in v. 5 to support the point that, ultimately, each person is responsible for himself or herself.

If 6:1–5 is linked to the mutual infighting among the Galatians engaged in theological conflict (5:15, 26), then 6:6–10 may be as well. Those who normally taught among the Galatian churches might have been deeply embroiled in the conflict. They were the most likely to consider themselves among the spiritual ones and to oppose the false teaching (6:1). Many of the ones who usually were taught by them were likely among those caught in the crossfire. In this situation, the support of the churches for their regular teachers may well have suffered.[69] So, it would make sense for Paul to exhort: "Furthermore [δέ], let the one who is instructed in the word share in all good things with the one who gives instruction" (6:6).

"Do not be deceived! God is not mocked" (6:7) grabs the audience's attention for what follows.[70] Paul introduces an agricultural principle that one will reap what one sows, which he applies to the final judgment.[71] "For [γὰρ] whatever a person sows, he or she will also reap. This means that [ὅτι] the one who sows to his or her own flesh will reap corruption from the flesh, but [δέ] the one who sows to the Spirit will reap eternal life from the Spirit" (6:7–8). With the context of 5:16–26 behind us, sowing to the Spirit is another way to refer to the same underlying reality as walking in the Spirit (5:16), being led by the Spirit (5:18), and walking in step with the Spirit (5:25). As such, those who sow to the Spirit will produce the fruit of the Spirit (5:22–23). They will practically serve one another through love by restoring those in need of restoration (6:1) and sharing good things with those who instruct them (6:6).[72] Those who sow to the Spirit will reap eternal life at the last judgment. This is connected to the future hoped-for righteousness believers still await (5:5). In contrast, those who sow to his or her own flesh will reap corruption. This refers to the opposite of eternal life, i.e., eternal judgment.[73] This recalls his declaration that those who practice the works of the flesh will not inherit the kingdom of God (5:21).

---

69. Similarly, DeSilva, *Galatians*, 490.

70. Similarly Runge, *Galatians*, Gal 6:1–10. I would also note the conceptual links that being deceived has to the scenarios Paul posed earlier about his opponents trying to confuse the Galatians and wanting to distort the gospel (1:7), having bewitched the Galatians (3:1), and infecting the Galatians with a persuasion that is not from God (5:8–9). It is also connected to Paul's earlier warning that those who practice what the flesh wants to do will not inherit the kingdom of God (5:21).

71. Schreiner, *Galatians*, 368.

72. Schreiner, *Galatians*, 369.

73. Moo, *Galatians*, s.vv. "The Urgency of Living the New Life" (Gal 6:7–10).

If the interpretation thus far is correct, Paul has first given two exhortations specific to the situation of the Galatians before now moving to a more general appeal that covers those situations: "In addition [δὲ], let us not lose heart in doing what is good. For [γὰρ] we will reap in due time, if we do not grow weary" (6:9). The emphasis is on persevering in doing good. The time that is appropriate for the harvest is coming. We will reap the harvest at God's final judgment.[74] The one who sows to the Spirit in v. 8 and those who do not lose heart in doing what is good in v. 9 will reap the harvest. This continuation of the harvest imagery connects sowing to the Spirit and doing what is good.[75] Sowing to the Spirit is, in turn, connected to the call to walk in step with the Spirit (5:16–26) and the specific commands to restore the fallen and support those who instruct them in the Word.

Why might the Galatians potentially lose heart and grow weary? The desires of their own flesh were constantly in a tug-of-war with the Spirit within them for their allegiance (5:17). False teachers were attempting to bewitch (3:1) them and were putting obstacles in their way (5:7). Within their communities, the works of the flesh were evident, with much division and infighting (5:15, 26). Some members had been overtaken by sin and required restoration (6:1). Some had to be encouraged to support their teachers (6:6). Nevertheless, if they persevere in the Spirit by faith, they will reap eternal life (6:8). They will obtain the hoped-for righteousness at the last day (5:5).

With strong inferential markers (Ἄρα οὖν), Paul encapsulates the main point of 6:1–10: "Therefore, while we have the opportunity, let us work what is good to all, especially to those who are members of the household of faith" (6:10). While different words are used, doing what is good (τὸ καλὸν ποιοῦντες) and working what is good (ἐργαζώμεθα τὸ ἀγαθὸν) should mean the same thing.[76] "While we have the opportunity" refers to as long as it is the season for sowing.[77] While v. 9 encourages perseverance by pointing to the final reward, v. 10 encourages taking advantage of the opportunity to continue to do good. Verse 10 also defines the recipients of the good they are to do. Generally, the recipients are all people without distinction. He also highlights the priority of their brothers and sisters in Christ.[78] As the sons and daughters of God through faith in Christ (3:26–29; 4:4–7), they are members of the same household of faith.

---

74. Moo, *Galatians*, s.vv. "The Urgency of Living the New Life" (Gal 6:7–10).
75. DeSilva, *Galatians*, 495.
76. Moo, *Galatians*, s.vv. "The Urgency of Living the New Life" (Gal 6:7–10).
77. DeSilva, *Galatians*, 496.
78. Similarly, Runge, *Galatians*, Gal 6:1–10.

It is noteworthy that working what is good (ἐργαζώμεθα τὸ ἀγαθὸν) leads to eternal life, where works of the law (ἔργα νόμου) led to a curse (3:10) and inability to be justified before God (2:16). Paul's previous association of the works of the flesh with the law as opposed to the Spirit with living by faith (3:2–3) still applies. We also should not forget about what Paul had said about waiting for the hope of righteousness through the Spirit by faith (5:5) as well as faith working through love having force (5:6). Likewise, working what is good is possible only by keeping in step with the Spirit (5:16, 18, 25).

GALATIANS 6:11–18

OUTLINE

II. First Round of Rebuke, Backed by Extended Support (1:6—2:21)

III. Second Round of Rebuke, Backed by Extended Support (3:1—4:7)

IV. Third Round of Rebuke (4:8–31)

V. Extended Exhortation with Fourth Round of Rebuke Embedded (5:1—6:10)

VI. Letter Closing (6:11–18)

    A. Parting Contrast Between Paul and the Opponents (6:11–17)

    B. Closing Benediction (6:18)

VI. LETTER CLOSING (6:11–18)

Table 33: The Flow of 6:11–18				
Connector	At	Connects	With	Function
None	6:11			Major break (starts letter closing)
Closely related concept	6:12a	6:12	1:6—6:10	Negative appraisal (of opponents)
μόνον ἵνα	6:12b	6:12b	6:12a	Purpose (of opponents)
γὰρ	6:13a	6:13	6:12	Supports (negative appraisal in 6:12)

ἀλλά	6:13b	6:13b-c	6:12–13a	Corrects (perceptions of opponents)
ἵνα	6:13c	6:13c	6:13b	Purpose (of opponents)
δέ	6:14a	6:14	6:12–13	Contrasts (with Paul's perspective)
Relative clause (2x)	6:14b-c	6:14b-c	6:14a	Defines (cross's impact)
γάρ	6:15a	6:15	6:14	Supports (cross's impact)
ἀλλά	6:15b	6:15b	6:15a	Corrects (perceptions of what matters)
καί	6:16	6:16	6:14–15	Associated (Paul's perspective)
Closely related concept	6:17a	6:17a	1:6—6:16	Closing request
γάρ	6:17b	6:17b	6:17a	Supports (Paul's closing request)
None	6:18	6:18	1:1—6:17	Minor break. Closing prayer wish

Weima has argued that Paul's letter closings are carefully constructed and connect directly to the letter's main points. They are like the thanksgivings in reverse: Whereas the thanksgiving previews the significant concerns the body will address, the closing underscores and summarizes those main points. Therefore, the closing offers interpretive clues that enrich our understanding of the letter.[1] So, what clues do we find in Galatians' letter closing?

A. Parting Contrast Between Paul and Opponents (6:11–17)

Compared with Paul's other letters, Galatians omits some things Paul commonly mentions in his letter closing. For example, Paul often includes greetings from his associates (Rom 16:16, 21-23; 1 Cor 16:19-20; 2 Cor 13:13; Phil 4:21-22; Col 4:10-14; 2 Tim 4:21; Titus 3:15; Phlm 23-24) and exhortations to greet one another (Rom 16:3-16; 1 Cor 16:20; 2 Cor 13:12; Phil 4:21; Col 4:15; 1 Thess 5:26; 2 Tim 4:19; Titus 3:15).[2] It seems that, like the omission of his usual thanksgiving after the letter opening, Paul dispensed with some of the usual polite features due to the specific situation

---

1. Weima, "Pauline Letter Closings," 184.
2. Moo has a helpful table of common letter closing features in Paul's letters (*Galatians*, s.vv. "Closing: Cross and New Creation" [Gal 6:11–18], "Additional Notes").

in Galatians. In 1:1–5 and 1:6—2:21, Paul has already reinforced the divine origin of his apostleship and message. In 3:1—4:7, he has effectively demonstrated that the real good news involves believing when hearing that message rather than getting circumcised and doing what the law requires. In 4:8–31, he further established how inconceivable it was for them to go back to slavery from the freedom they already enjoyed. At this point, Paul has already built an overwhelming case to back his call to the Galatians to stand firm and not be subject again to a yoke of slavery (5:1). He has also offered the Galatians a positive solution on how to complete the journey that they had started, which is to walk in step with the Spirit they had received when they believed Paul's message. Moreover, they can be assured that they will not fulfill the desire of the flesh when they do so.

Even with both these main points already powerfully made, Paul chooses to highlight once more the need to repudiate his opponents and to boast only in the cross of Christ.[3] How does Paul accomplish this task? He connects and contrasts these opponents and their message to the positive portrait already established for Paul and his message. Just as Paul starts the letter by putting forth his credentials, he ends by discrediting his opponents. If you should trust Paul and shun his disreputable opponents, obviously you should follow his message rather than theirs. So, even in this letter closing, Paul continues to put the finishing touches on his exhortation to his audience to stand firm in the true gospel and reject the false one that brings slavery. Throughout this chapter, I will purposely and painstakingly recapitulate connections to significant concerns throughout the letter. At the risk of sounding repetitive, this exercise will help to paint a fuller picture of the overall connections.

Paul concludes at least some of his letters in his own hand (1 Cor 16:21; Col 4:18; 2 Thess 3:17; Phlm 19).[4] In Galatians, he draws extra attention to the letter closing:[5] "See with what large letters I am writing to you in my own hand!" (6:11). He not only uses an attention marker, "See!" (ἴδετε), but also emphasizes both the size of his writing and the fact that he wrote this extra-long closing in his own hand.[6] In so doing, he highlights the contrast

---

3. Weima, *Neglected Endings*, 159–60.
4. Schreiner, *Galatians*, 376.
5. Weima, "Gal 6:11–18," 90–91.
6. Runge, *Galatians*, Gal 6:11–18. Levinsohn cites the lack of conjunction, the attention marker "see!," the change from first-person plural to first-person singular, and a summary statement in 6:10 that closes that section as evidence of a major division at 6:11 ("Galatians," 309). The typical view is that Paul usually uses a co-worker or scribe (functioning essentially as an secretary) to write his letters and that he only personally wrote the closings where he called attention to writing in his own hand. DeSilva argues

he is about to draw between himself and his opponents: those who want to make a good showing in the flesh try to compel you to be circumcised, only so that they will not be persecuted because of the cross of Christ (6:12). He explains further: "For [γὰρ] those who are circumcised[7] do not keep the law themselves, but they want you to be circumcised so that they might boast in your flesh" (6:13).

Paul's opponents want to boast in the Galatians' flesh (6:13). By making a good showing in the flesh (with the gentile Galatians circumcised), they would be able to avoid persecution because of the cross of Christ (6:12). Avoidance of persecution is the real motive for their trying to force the Galatians to be circumcised. It is not because they want others to keep the law or even keep it themselves (6:13). As Paul has already warned, if the Galatians accept circumcision, they would, in effect, be taking on the keeping of the Jewish law. Every man who receives circumcision is a debtor to do the whole law (5:2–3). They cannot live by doing the works of the law (3:10–12). This is because everyone who relies on the works of the law is cursed for failing to do everything written in the book of the law. This likely is what Paul had in mind when he claimed that his opponents do not keep the law themselves. It is because no one is justified before God by means of the law (3:11).[8]

As previously noted, the common theme of compelling (ἀναγκάζω) gentile believers to be circumcised draws a comparison of these opponents both to the false brothers in 2:3–5 and to Cephas (who had to be rebuked and corrected) in 2:14. There Paul challenged Cephas for hypocrisy when he knew better. Here, too, Paul appears to imply that these opponents know better. At least they know enough to distort the gospel (1:6–7) into a message that achieves their purpose of not being persecuted because of the cross of Christ. In Gal 5:11, Paul had previously linked circumcision with persecution. Paul was being persecuted precisely because he no longer advocated circumcision. This was because advocating circumcision nullifies the significance of Christ crucified. As previously noted, the heart of the issue seems to be gentiles being accepted into God's family on equal terms with Jews through faith in the crucified Messiah, without requiring circumcision and keeping of the Jewish law. Their agenda of trying to force the gentile Galatian Christians to be circumcised (6:12, reinforced by "they want you

---

plausibly that Paul calling attention to his own handwriting here need not mean that he did not write everything before the closing (*Galatians*, 502–5).

7. The witnesses are divided between the present participle and the perfect participle. The present participle is the preferred reading, but both would refer to those who are circumcised. See Moo, *Galatians*, s.vv. "Closing: Cross and New Creation" (Gal 6:11–18), "Additional Notes."

8. Similarly, Moo, *Galatians*, s.vv. "Closing: Cross and New Creation" (Gal 6:11–18).

to be circumcised" [6:13]) directly avoids the stumbling block of the cross (5:11). Circumcising the Galatians allows them to make a good showing in the flesh (6:12). They can boast in the flesh of the Galatians, i.e., claim honor (likely in the eyes of fellow Jews) through the circumcised flesh of the Galatians (6:13).[9] Non-Christian Jews would be less likely to persecute them if Christianity was seen as a Jewish sect where Jewish Christians continued to keep the Jewish law while bringing gentiles in to do the same.[10]

However (δέ), as for Paul: "May it never be that I should boast, except in the cross of our Lord Jesus Christ, through which the world has been crucified to me and I to the world" (6:14). "For [γὰρ] neither circumcision nor uncircumcision is anything, but [ἀλλὰ] a new creation [—that is something!]" (6:15).

Paul encapsulates much of what he has already established previously. First, why is it that neither circumcision nor uncircumcision is anything? Just like everyone else, even Jewish Christians must be justified through faith in Christ and not through the works of the law (2:16). Jews and Greeks alike are sons of God through faith in Christ Jesus (3:26–29). In Christ Jesus neither circumcision nor uncircumcision has any force, but faith working through love has force (5:6).[11] The parallel dismissal of the relevance of the state of being circumcised (for Jews) or being uncircumcised (for gentiles) in 5:6 and 6:15 is particularly striking. The new creation thus appears to be related to being sons of God through faith in Christ and faith working through love.[12] Those who are in Christ live through the Spirit by faith. Christ lives in them as they live by faith in Christ (2:20). Christ is being formed in them (4:19). Through the Spirit by faith they wait for the hope of righteousness (5:5). They walk in step with the Spirit and work what is good out of the fruit of the Spirit, with love for one's neighbor at the forefront (5:16—6:10)

Because Paul knows the significance of the new creation, he will boast only in the cross of our Lord Jesus Christ. But why the cross? Through Christ's crucifixion, the world has been crucified to Paul and Paul to the world. Christ gave himself for them on the cross to rescue them from this present evil age (1:4).[13] As Paul has previously outlined in 2:19–20, through

---

9. DeSilva, *Galatians*, 508; Schreiner, *Galatians*, 377.

10. Similarly, DeSilva, *Galatians*, 505.

11. Many witnesses add "in Christ Jesus" and replace the verb "is" with "has force" in 6:15 (likely assimilated to 5:6).

12. Similarly, DeSilva, *Galatians*, 510–11. Schreiner also points out the parallel to 1 Cor 7:19, where neither circumcision nor uncircumcision matters, but rather keeping God's commands (*Galatians*, 380).

13. As Moo notes, the new creation stands in contrast to the "world" (v. 14 [2x]) and "the present evil age" (1:4) (*Galatians*, s.vv. "Closing: Cross and New Creation" [Gal 6:11–18]).

their union with Christ by faith, they are considered crucified together with Christ.[14] The law cursed Christ and condemned him to death for the sins of those united with him (3:13). They are considered to have died together with Christ on the cross. Together with Christ, they are considered dead to the law and are no longer obligated to it. They (in the sense of their human condition limited by sin) no longer live (2:19–20). In addition, together with Christ, they are considered to have crucified the flesh and its passion and desires (5:24). This new state of affairs also includes no longer being under the custody of the law (3:23–25) and redemption from being enslaved to the law and other elementary principles of the world, which include idols (4:1–11).[15] Even divisive religious, social, and sexual pairs of opposites are no longer relevant (3:26–29). In effect, the world has been crucified as far as believers are concerned, and believers have been crucified as far as the world is concerned (6:14–15). This is consistent with Paul's similar statements in 2 Cor 5:14–21.

DeSilva comments similarly, with an eloquent paragraph that I would like to quote in full here:

> Paul challenges us to embrace the freedom and the challenge of living by the Spirit, trusting this gift of God to bring us fully in line with the character and standards of God and to transform us into the likeness of Jesus, the image of the Father. He challenges us to use this freedom responsibly, as spiritual adults. Christian freedom is never an occasion for self-serving, but always an occasion to serve and to love beyond the limits set on us by our upbringing, our socialization, our customs—in short, by the "world" (6:14). The righteousness that God seeks to impart will be manifested in the character of our Christian community. Are we other-centered or self-centered? Are we marked by cooperation or by competition? Do we live out the vision where, indeed, ethnic, social, and gender distinctions—and the hierarchical evaluations, limitations, abuses, or avoidances that are fostered by such distinctions—are transcended in the one family of God's children and heirs? Only by following the Spirit will we, as a Christian community, arrive at the full freedom and glorious inheritance of the sons and daughters of God.[16]

Paul adds: "And [καὶ] for those who shall keep in step with this rule, may peace and mercy be upon them, even upon the Israel of God" (6:16).

---

14. Moo, *Galatians*, s.vv. "Closing: Cross and New Creation" (Gal 6:11–18).
15. Similarly, Schreiner, *Galatians*, 379.
16. DeSilva, *Galatians*, 517.

This prayer wish is for those who will walk by the rule he just expressed in 6:15, namely that the new creation is what matters, while circumcision and uncircumcision are irrelevant. By using the same verb (στοιχέω), Paul links those who walk in step with the rule of the new creation with those who walk in step with the Spirit (5:25). This is consistent with how Isa 32:12–18 had previously connected the Spirit with the new age.[17]

What is the relationship between those who walk by this rule and the Israel of God? While the matter is disputed, the context of the letter supports identifying them as all who walk by this rule, both believing gentiles and believing Jews. First, Paul just asserted that circumcision and uncircumcision are irrelevant in the immediately prior verse. Second, Paul redefined Abraham's offspring and established that only those who rely on faith in Christ (not biological descendants) are Abraham's true heirs (3:7—4:7). Third, like Isaac, they are children of promise (4:28). Their (and Paul's)[18] mother is the Jerusalem above (4:26), not the present Jerusalem that is enslaved together with her children (4:25). The Israel of God then refers to the same underlying reality as the new creation. They are the new household of faith that consists of Abraham's true heirs. They are the children of promise whose mother is the Jerusalem above. So, all who walk in step with the rule that the new creation is what matters rather than circumcision or uncircumcision (i.e., all believers in Christ) are members of the true Israel, God's Israel.[19]

As a closing request, Paul asks: "From now on, let no one lay any further burdens on me." Now that the new creation has come (v. 16), no one should try to impose the elements (4:3, 9) that belong to the present evil age (1:4) on him or his converts.[20] The reason he cites is as follows: "For [γὰρ] I myself carry the brand marks of Jesus in my body" (6:17). In 1:13—2:21, Paul has already furnished abundant evidence that he is Christ's slave and preached a divine rather than human gospel. This included independence from potential human authorities and the willingness to confront and correct them. Unlike his opponents who avoided persecution for the cross of Christ (6:12–13), he experienced persecution precisely for upholding the truth of the gospel of the crucified Messiah and no longer advocating circumcision (5:11). The marks on his body from facing hostility and beatings are physical evidence of his unassailable credibility.[21]

---

17. Schreiner, *Galatians*, 380.

18. Paul uses an inclusive "our."

19. Similarly, Moo, *Galatians*, s.vv. "Closing: Cross and New Creation" (Gal 6:11–18); Schreiner, *Galatians*, 382–83; DeSilva, *Galatians*, 512–13.

20. Schreiner, *Galatians*, 383–84.

21. DeSilva, *Galatians*, 514–15.

B. Closing Benediction (6:18)

Paul ends by praying that the grace of Christ will be with the spirits of the Galatian Christians. A prayer wish is typical at or near the conclusion of Paul's letters (Rom 16:20; 1 Cor 16:23; 2 Cor 13:14; Eph 6:24; Phil 4:23; Col 4:18; 1 Thess 5:28; 2 Thess 3:18; 1 Tim 6:21; 2 Tim 4:22; Titus 3:15; Phlm 25). Paul's grace benediction in Galatians comes closest to the one in Phil 4:23 and Phlm 25. In comparison with these other prayer wishes, three things stand out. First, Paul may be adding inclusive "our" (ἡμῶν) to "our Lord Jesus Christ" to emphasize that he views the Galatians as genuinely belonging to Jesus. Second, he again addressed the Galatians as "brothers and sisters" at the end of the letter. This may also assure them that Paul sees them as fellow members of the household of faith. Finally, Paul adds a final "amen," which he usually does not use with his closing prayer wishes. The "amen" confirms and ratifies his prayer.[22] After spending the whole letter rebuking the Galatians for rejecting God's grace in Christ and giving them a new appreciation for it, Paul fittingly concludes by praying that God will continue to pour this grace into their lives.[23]

---

22. Schreiner, *Galatians*, 384–85.

23. Longenecker suggests that this grace benediction in Galatians is especially meaningful. The opening salutation in 1:3 describes grace from God our Father and the Lord Jesus Christ, and the closing benediction in 6:18 mentions the grace of our Lord Jesus Christ. In between, Paul refers to the Galatians being called by the grace of Christ (1:6). Paul himself is called by God's grace (1:15). The Jerusalem apostles recognized the grace given him by God (2:9). Unlike Cephas and other Jewish Christians led astray by him, Paul did not reject God's grace (2:21). God also "graciously gave" (verbal cognate) the inheritance to Abraham through a promise (3:18) (*Galatians*, 300).

BIBLIOGRAPHY

Arichea, Daniel C., and Eugene A. Nida. *A Translator's Handbook on Paul's Letter to the Galatians*. New York: United Bible Societies, 1976.
Armitage, David J. "An Exploration of Conditional Clause Exegesis with Reference to Galatians 1, 8–9." *Bib* 88 (2007) 365–92.
Barclay, John M. G. "Mirror-Reading a Polemical Letter: Galatians as Test Case." *Journal for the Study of the New Testament* 31 (1987) 73–93.
Barr, James. *The Semantics of Biblical Language*. Oxford: Oxford University Press, 1961.
Bauer, Laurie. *The Linguistics Student's Handbook*. Edinburgh: Edinburgh University Press, 2007.
Beekman, John, and John Callow. *Translating the Word of God*. Dallas: SIL International, 2002.
Betz, Hans D. *Galatians: A Commentary on Paul's Letter to the Churches in Galatia*. Hermeneia. Philadelphia: Fortress, 1979.
Black, Stephanie. *Sentence Conjunctions in the Gospel of Matthew: καί, δέ, τότε, γάρ, οὖν and Asyndeton in Narrative Discourse*. Sheffield: Sheffield Academic, 2002.
Blight, Richard C. *Exegetical Helps on Galatians*. Dallas: SIL International, 2003.
Breeze, Mary. "Hortatory Discourse in Ephesians." *Journal of Translation and Textlinguistics* 5 (1992) 313–37.
Bruce, F. F. *The Epistle to the Galatians: A Commentary on the Greek Text*. NIGTC. Exeter, UK: Paternoster, 1982.
Callow, Kathleen. *Man and Message*. Lanham, MD: University Press of America, 1998. E-book.
DeSilva, David A. *The Letter to the Galatians*. NICNT. Grand Rapids: Eerdmans, 2018.
Fung, Ronald Y. K. *The Epistle to the Galatians*. NICNT. Grand Rapids: Eerdmans, 1988.
George, Timothy. *Galatians*. NAC. Nashville: Broadman & Holman, 1994.
Granger, Sylviane, and Fanny Meunier, eds. *Phraseology: An Interdisciplinary Perspective*. Amsterdam: Benjamins, 2008.
Greaves, Chris, and Martin Warren. "What Can a Corpus Tell Us About Multi-Word Units?" In *The Routledge Handbook of Corpus Linguistics*, edited by Anne O'Keeffe and Michael J. McCarthy, 204–20. Routledge Handbooks in Applied Linguistics. London: Routledge, 2022.
Halliday, M. A. K. *Halliday's Introduction to Functional Grammar*. Revised by Christian M. I. M. Matthiessen. 4th ed. London: Routledge, 2013.

———. "Introduction: On the 'Architecture' of Human Language." In *On Language and Linguistics*, edited by Jonathan J. Webster, 1–32. Vol. 3 of *Collected Works of M. A. K. Halliday*. London: Continuum, 2003.

———. "Language Structure and Language Function." In *New Horizons in Linguistics*, edited by John Lyons, 140–65. Harmondsworth, UK: Penguin, 1970.

Halliday, M. A. K., and Ruqaiya Hasan. *Cohesion in English*. London: Longman, 1976.

Hardin, Justin K. "Galatians 1–2 Without a Mirror: Reflections on Paul's Conflict with the Agitators." *Tyndale Bulletin* 65 (2014) 275–303.

Hasan, Ruqaiya. "The Grammarian's Dream: Lexis as Most Delicate Grammar." In *New Developments in Systemic Linguistics*, edited by M. A. K. Halliday and Robin P. Fawcett, 1:184–211. London: Pinter, 1987.

Hasselgård, Hilde, et al., eds. *Corpus Perspectives on Patterns of Lexis*. Amsterdam: Benjamins, 2013.

Herbst, Thomas, et al., eds. *The Phraseological View of Language: A Tribute to John Sinclair*. Berlin: de Gruyter, 2013.

Hong, In-Gyu. *The Law in Galatians*. Journal for the Study of the New TestamentSup 81. Sheffield: Sheffield Academic, 1993.

Jervis, L. Ann. *The Purpose of Romans: A Comparative Letter Structure Investigation*. LNTS. London: Bloomsbury, 1991.

Keener, Craig S. *Galatians: A Commentary*. Grand Rapids: Baker Academic, 2019. E-book.

Kirk, Alexander. "New Testament Argument Diagramming: A Proposal for a Modified Analytical Technique." AWS, Dec. 21, 2009. https://s3.amazonaws.com/cdn.gospelpaths.com/tenants/5/1562079650143-New%20Testament%20Argument%20Diagramming.pdf.

Levinsohn, Stephen H. "Discourse Analysis: Galatians as a Case Study." In *Linguistics and New Testament Greek: Key Issues in the Current Debate*, edited by David Alan Black and Benjamin L. Merkle, 103–24. Grand Rapids: Baker Academic, 2020.

———. *Discourse Features of New Testament Greek: A Coursebook on the Information Structure of New Testament Greek*. 2nd ed. Dallas: Summer Institute of Linguistics, 2000. E-book.

———. "Galatians." In *Discourse Analysis of the New Testament Writings*, edited by Todd A. Scacewater, 207–330. Dallas: Fontes, 2020.

Lightfoot, Joseph B. *St. Paul's Epistle to the Galatians*. 10th ed. London: Macmillan, 1890.

Longacre, Robert E. "Exhortation and Mitigation in First John." *Selected Technical Articles Related to Translation* 9 (1983) 3–44.

Longenecker, Richard N. *Galatians*. WBC. Dallas: Word, 1990.

Mann, William C., and Sandra A. Thompson. *Rhetorical Structure Theory: A Theory of Text Organization*. Technical Report ISI/RS-87-190. Marina del Rey, CA: Information Sciences Institute Press, 1987.

———. "Rhetorical Structure Theory: Toward a Functional Theory of Text Organization." *Text—Interdisciplinary Journal for the Study of Discourse* 8 (1988) 243–81.

Martyn, J. Louis. *Galatians: A New Translation with Introduction and Commentary*. AYB. New Haven, CT: Yale University Press, 2008.

Moo, Douglas J. *Galatians*. BECNT. Grand Rapids: Baker Academic, 2013. E-book.

Neeley, Linda. "A Discourse Analysis of Hebrews." *Occasional Papers in Translation and Textlinguistics* 1 (1987) 1–146.

Nicolle, Steve. "Conditionals in Galatians: A Guide for Translators." *Journal of Translation* 18 (2022) 89–113.

O'Brien, Peter. *Introductory Thanksgivings in the Letters of Paul*. NovTSup 49. Leiden: Brill, 1977.

Parunak, H. Van Dyke. "Dimensions of Discourse Structure: A Multidimensional Analysis of the Components and Transitions of Paul's Epistle to the Galatians." In *Linguistics and New Testament Interpretation: Essays on Discourse Analysis*, edited by David Alan Black, et al., 207–39. Nashville: Broadman, 1992.

Porter, Stanley E. *Idioms of the Greek New Testament*. 2nd ed. Sheffield: Sheffield Academic, 1999.

———. *Linguistic Analysis of the Greek New Testament: Studies in Tools, Methods, and Practice*. Grand Rapids: Baker Academic, 2015.

Porter, Stanley E., and Andrew W. Pitts. "Πίστις with a Preposition and Genitive Modifier: Lexical, Semantic, and Syntactic Considerations in the Πίστις Χριστοῦ Discussion." In *The Faith of Jesus Christ: Exegetical, Biblical, and Theological Studies*, edited by Michael F. Bird and Preston M. Sprinkle, 33–53. Milton Keynes, UK: Paternoster, 2009.

Porter, Stanley E., and Matthew Brook O'Donnell. "Conjunctions, Clines and Levels of Discourse." *Filología Neotestamentaria* 20 (2007) 3–14.

———. *Discourse Analysis and the Greek New Testament: Text-Generating Resources*. T&T Clark Library of New Testament Greek. London: T&T Clark, 2024.

Reed, Jeffrey T. *A Discourse Analysis of Philippians: Method and Rhetoric in the Debate over Literary Integrity*. LNTS. Sheffield: Sheffield Academic, 1997.

Runge, Steven E. *Discourse Grammar of the Greek New Testament: A Practical Introduction for Teaching and Exegesis*. Bellingham, WA: Lexham, 2010. E-book.

———. *Galatians*. High Definition Commentary. Bellingham, WA: Lexham, 2019. E-book.

———. *The Lexham Discourse Greek New Testament*. Bellingham, WA: Lexham, 2008–14. E-book.

Schnabel, Eckhard J. *Paul and the Early Church*. Vol. 2 of *Early Christian Mission*. Downers Grove, IL: InterVarsity, 2004.

Schreiner, Thomas R. *Galatians*. ZECNT. Grand Rapids: Zondervan, 2010.

———. *Interpreting the Pauline Epistles*. 2nd ed. Grand Rapids: Baker, 2011.

Silva, Moisés. *Interpreting Galatians: Explorations in Exegetical Method*. 2nd ed. Grand Rapids: Baker, 2001.

Simpson, James. "Introduction: Applied Linguistics in the Contemporary World." In *The Routledge Handbook of Applied Linguistics*, edited by James Simpson, 1–7. Routledge Handbooks in Applied Linguistics. London: Routledge, 2011.

Symphony Browser. https://symphony.clearlabs.biblica.com/.

Taboada, Maite, and William C. Mann. "Rhetorical Structure Theory: Looking Back and Moving Ahead." *Discourse Studies* 8 (2006) 423–59.

Tan, Randall K. J. "Linguistics and Biblical Studies: An Ongoing Journey." In *Linguistics and the Bible: Retrospect and Prospects*, edited by Stanley E. Porter et al., 9–27. MNTS 9. Eugene, OR: Pickwick, 2019.

Van Voorst, Robert E. "Why Is There No Thanksgiving Period in Galatians? An Assessment of an Exegetical Commonplace." *Journal of Biblical Literature* 129 (2010) 153–72.

Verster, Pieter. "The Implications of Nonauthentic Questions in Galatians." Supplement 9, *AcT* 28 (2008) 142–61. http://doi.org/10.4314/actat.v28i2.52344.

Weima, Jeffrey A. D. "Gal 6:11–18: A Hermeneutical Key to the Galatian Letter." *Calvin Theological Journal* 28 (1993) 90–107.

———. *Neglected Endings: The Significance of Pauline Letter Closings*. Journal for the Study of the New TestamentSup 101. Sheffield: Sheffield Academic, 1994.

———. "The Pauline Letter Closings: Analysis and Hermeneutical Significance." *Bulletin for Biblical Research* 5 (1995) 177–98.

Wiarda, Timothy. "Plot and Character in Galatians 1–2." *Tyndale Bulletin* 55 (2004) 231–52.

Yoon, David I. *A Discourse Analysis of Galatians and the New Perspective on Paul*. LBS 17. Leiden: Brill, 2019.

———. "Discourse Analysis and the Textual Metafunction: Analyzing the Texture of Galatians 4,12–20." *Filología Neotestamentaria* 27 (2014) 83–110.

———. "Identifying the End of Paul's Speech to Peter in Galatians 2: Register Analysis as a Heuristic Tool." *Filología Neotestamentaria* 28–29 (2015–2016) 57–79.

———. "Prominence in New Testament Discourse: Galatians 1,11–2,10 as a Test Case." *Filología Neotestamentaria* 26 (2013) 3–26.

———. "The Transitivity Network and Koine Greek: The (Ideational) Meaning of Galatians 3:1—5:1." *Biblical and Ancient Greek Linguistics* 8 (2019) 79–110.

Zeldes, Amir, et al. "eRST: A Signaled Graph Theory of Discourse Relations and Organization." *arXiv* (2024) https://doi.org/10.48550/arXiv.2403.13560.

MODERN AUTHOR INDEX

Arichea, Daniel C., 44
Armitage, David J., 46

Barclay, John M. G., 44
Barr, James, 4
Bauer, Laurie, 2
Beekman, John, 16, 17
Betz, Hans D., 81
Black, Stephanie, 18
Blight, Richard C., 47
Breeze, Mary, 49
Bruce, F. F., 53, 60, 71, 72, 85, 86, 106

Callow, John, 4, 6, 16, 17, 18, 64, 80, 93
Callow, Kathleen, 4, 8, 10, 11, 12, 15, 16, 39

DeSilva, David A., 27, 28, 31, 36, 40, 41, 46, 47, 48, 49, 53, 54, 55, 59, 61, 72, 73, 78, 84, 90, 91, 93, 94, 95, 96, 97, 103, 105, 106, 107, 108, 109, 111, 112, 113, 114, 117, 118, 119, 123, 125, 126, 127

Fung, Ronald Y. K., 51

George, Timothy, 27, 52, 53
Granger, Sylviane, 4
Greaves, Chris, 4

Halliday, M. A. K., 6, 7, 8, 18
Hardin, Justin K., 44, 48
Hasan, Ruqaiya, 4, 18
Hasselgård, Hilde, 4

Herbst, Thomas, 4
Hong, In-Gyu, 82

Jervis, L. Ann, 5, 40

Keener, Craig S., 62, 65, 111
Kirk, Alexander, 6

Levinsohn, Stephen H., 5, 15, 18, 21, 38, 46, 47, 48, 49, 66, 68, 72, 73, 74, 75, 76, 79, 80, 82, 84, 91, 92, 93, 96, 116, 123
Lightfoot, Joseph B., 117
Longacre, Robert E., 16
Longenecker, Richard N., 47, 52, 53, 57, 60, 66, 75, 85, 90, 106, 128

Mann, William C., 6, 12, 13, 17, 19
Martyn, J. Louis, 82
Meunier, Fanny, 4
Moo, Douglas J., 26, 28, 31, 32, 35, 36, 40, 41, 44, 48, 50, 52, 56, 57, 58, 59, 60, 63, 66, 67, 71, 72, 75, 76, 80, 81, 84, 85, 87, 89, 93, 97, 98, 102, 104, 105, 106, 108, 109, 111, 112, 116, 118, 119, 122, 124, 125, 126, 127

Neeley, Linda, 16
Nicolle, Steve, 45, 46, 48, 63, 65, 66, 67, 73, 83, 86, 93, 107, 114

O'Brien, Peter, 11, 40

O'Donnell, Matthew Brook, 2, 3, 6, 7, 8, 9, 10, 11, 12, 14, 15, 16, 19, 20, 21, 28

Parunak, H. Van Dyke, 51, 62
Pitts, Andrew W., 65
Porter, Stanley E., 2, 3, 6, 7, 8, 9, 10, 11, 12, 14, 15, 16, 19, 20, 21, 28, 65

Reed, Jeffrey T., 6, 9, 28
Runge, Steven E., 5, 7, 17, 18, 28, 31, 35, 41, 42, 44, 45, 49, 52, 53, 54, 57, 58, 60, 61, 62, 63, 64, 68, 70, 72, 73, 84, 89, 96, 97, 103, 104, 107, 109, 111, 112, 113, 116, 117, 118, 119, 123

Schnabel, Eckhard J., 57
Schreiner, Thomas R., 6, 17, 27, 28, 32, 45, 48, 49, 52, 53, 55, 56, 58, 59, 60, 61, 62, 64, 72, 76, 78, 79, 80, 82, 83, 103, 104, 106, 108, 112, 113, 114, 116, 117, 118, 123, 125, 126, 127, 128

Seifrid, Mark, 63
Silva, Moisés, 44, 73
Simpson, James, 3

Taboada, Maite, 12, 13, 17, 19
Tan, Randall K. J., 2
Thompson, Sandra A., 6, 13, 17

Van Voorst, Robert E., 26, 28, 40
Verster, Pieter, 48, 64

Warren, Martin, 4
Weima, Jeffrey A. D., 122, 123
Wiarda, Timothy, 54

Yoon, David I., 40, 51, 60, 64, 68, 81, 90, 93, 94, 114

Zeldes, Amir, 6, 13

SCRIPTURE INDEX

Genesis
11:30	97
12:1–3	78
12:3	75, 98
15:1–5	78
15:4	96
17:4–8	78
17:9–14	58
17:16	96
17:18–19	97
18:14	96
18:18	75, 78, 98
21:1–2	96
21:6–7	97
21:9	98
22:17–18	78
26:3–4	78
28:13–15	78
35:11–12	78

Leviticus
18:5	75, 96, 108

Deuteronomy
21:23	76
23:2	107
27:26	75, 96

Isaiah
32:12–18	127
49:1	52
52:13—53:12	97
54:1	97, 98

Jeremiah
1:5	52

Habakkuk
2:4	75

Matthew
7:5	117
15:19	112
22:39	117

Mark
12:31	117

Luke
10:27	117

John
13:34–35	117
15:12–17	117

Acts
5:34–40	27
9:1–19	27
9:1–2	27
9:11	27

Acts (continued)

9:26–29	32
11:25–26	55
11:27–30	32, 57, 61
12:25	32
13–14	32
13:9	27
15	32, 57
15:1–29	32
15:1	58, 59
15:5	58, 59
16:6	31
18:23	31
20	63
21:10	98
21:12	98
21:39	27
22:1–21	27
22:3	27
22:4–5	27
23:6	27
26:1–23	27

Romans

1:1	52
1:7	34
1:8	40
1:9	54
1:29	112
9:1	54
10:16	72
10:17	72
15:26	61
16:3–16	122
16:16	122
16:20	128
16:21–23	122

1 Corinthians

1:1	27, 31
1:3	34
6:9–10	112
7:19	125
9:26	57
15:8–10	51
16:19–20	122
16:20	122
16:21	123
16:23	128

2 Corinthians

1:1	27, 31
1:2	34
1:23	54
5:14–21	126
13:12	122
13:13	122
13:14	128

Galatians

1:1–5	21, 22, 25–36, 99, 123
1:1–2	23, 26–34
1:1	28, 35, 48, 49, 53
1:2	31, 42, 45
1:3–5	23
1:3–4	35
1:3	34, 41, 67, 128
1:4	34, 35, 36, 76, 125, 127
1:5	36, 40
1:6—4:31	102
1:6—2:21	21, 23, 37–67, 69, 99, 123
1:6–12	47
1:6–9	23, 36, 38, 39–46, 47, 49, 68, 107
1:6–7	23, 34, 40–44, 59, 94, 124
1:6	39, 40, 41, 46, 49, 52, 53, 55, 57, 67, 104, 106
1:7–9	39
1:7	39, 40, 41, 43, 49, 53, 55, 57, 71, 94, 106, 118
1:8–9	23, 39, 40, 44–46, 59, 71, 94, 106
1:8	40, 45, 47, 49, 53, 55, 57

SCRIPTURE INDEX

1:9	38, 40, 45, 46, 47, 49, 53, 55, 57	2:3	56, 58, 64, 103
		2:4	59, 60, 94, 97, 102
1:10—2:21	23, 30, 36, 46–67, 68, 93	2:5	60, 63, 94, 105
		2:6	32, 56, 58, 60, 117
1:10–12	38, 47	2:7–9	32, 61, 103
1:10	23, 40, 46, 47–48, 49, 102	2:7–8	54
		2:7	58, 60
1:10a–b	48	2:8	58
1:10c	48	2:9	56, 58, 60, 128
1:11—2:21	28	2:10	61
1:11—2:10	60	2:11–21	23, 30, 38, 46, 51, 58, 61–67
1:11–12	23, 40, 46, 49, 50, 53	2:11–14	64
1:11	34, 42, 46, 47, 49, 52, 53, 55, 57	2:11	38, 51, 62, 66
		2:12	51, 58, 62, 63
1:12	35, 46, 47, 49, 52	2:13	63
1:13—2:21	23, 32, 33, 38, 47, 50–67, 127	2:14–21	31, 62
		2:14	59, 63, 92, 94, 105, 124
1:13—2:14	47	2:15–21	66
1:13—2:10	46, 51	2:15	27, 63, 64, 65, 92
1:13–24	54	2:16	63, 64, 65, 71, 74, 81, 92, 104, 105, 107, 120, 125
1:13–17	23, 38, 50, 51–54, 63		
1:13–14	50, 107	2:17–18	92
1:13	27, 46, 47, 50, 51, 52, 54, 55, 63, 98	2:17	64, 65
		2:18–21	31
1:14	27, 52	2:18	66
1:15–17	50, 51, 53, 56	2:19–21	36, 66, 92, 109, 113
1:15–16	27, 35	2:19–20	125, 126
1:15	52, 128	2:19	66, 85, 92
1:16	27, 49, 52, 53, 54, 55, 57	2:20	36, 66, 67, 94, 105, 111, 117
1:17	51, 53	2:21—3:21	67
1:18–20	23, 50, 53, 54, 56, 63	2:21	36, 67, 71, 81, 92, 104, 128
1:18–19	32		
1:18	38, 51, 54, 56, 57	3:1—4:7	21, 23, 68–86, 99, 109, 123
1:19	54		
1:20	54	3	68
1:21–24	23, 51, 55, 63	3:1–14	73
1:21	38, 51, 55, 56	3:1–6	23, 69, 70–73, 105, 106
1:22	55		
1:23	55, 57, 98, 107	3:1–5	42, 68, 69, 73, 74, 75, 88
1:24	55		
2:1–21	63	3:1–4	73
2:1–10	23, 32, 51, 57, 56–61, 63	3:1	33, 42, 44, 68, 71, 72, 76, 78, 107, 118, 119
2:1–2	53		
2:1	38, 51, 56	3:2–5	111
2:2	51, 57, 58, 60, 90, 117		
2:3–5	64, 124		

Galatians (continued)

3:2–4	73
3:2–3	73, 120
3:2	72, 73, 74, 75, 76, 90, 104, 112
3:3	70, 72, 104, 105, 112, 113
3:4	73, 78, 90
3:5	72, 73, 74, 75, 76
3:6–9	89
3:6	70, 73, 74, 75, 104
3:7—4:7	23, 42, 71, 73–86, 87, 89, 90, 97, 107, 112, 127
3:7–14	23, 70, 71, 74–77, 89
3:7–12	76
3:7–9	75, 83
3:7	74, 75, 96
3:8	76, 98
3:9	75, 76
3:10–14	36
3:10–12	89, 124
3:10	75, 76, 96, 104, 120
3:11	75, 76, 81, 104, 124
3:12	75, 96, 104
3:13–14	76, 85, 89, 98, 102, 106
3:13	76, 78, 85, 89, 92, 107, 113, 126
3:14	73, 78, 81, 89, 92, 104, 113
3:15—4:7	23, 77–86, 89, 92, 107
3:15–18	23, 70, 77–79, 89, 90, 97
3:15–17	80
3:15–16	79
3:15	34, 42, 78, 84
3:17	79, 80, 104
3:18	77, 79, 80, 128
3:19–22	24, 70, 79–81, 90
3:19	80, 81, 82
3:20	80
3:21	67, 80, 81, 82
3:22–25	89
3:22	77, 81, 82, 94
3:23–29	24, 70, 81–83, 84, 90
3:23–25	82, 84, 106, 126
3:23	82, 92, 94
3:24	82, 92, 104
3:25	82, 92
3:26–29	36, 98, 105, 119, 125
3:26	82, 89
3:27–29	104
3:27	42, 83
3:28–29	84
3:28	83, 102
3:29	77, 79, 83, 84, 89, 96
4:1–11	36
4:1–7	24, 70, 77, 83–86, 89, 90, 97, 102, 112
4:1	84, 89, 102
4:2	36, 84
4:3–6	104
4:3–5	97
4:3	85, 90, 114, 127
4:4–7	71, 98, 119
4:4–5	85
4:4	36, 85
4:5–7	77, 89
4:5	89, 102
4:6–7	111
4:6	85, 86, 104
4:7	86, 89, 102
4:8–31	21, 24, 87–98, 99, 123
4:8–11	24, 87, 88, 89–90, 97, 102
4:8–9	42, 73, 87, 88, 89, 102, 108
4:8	90
4:9	90, 114, 127
4:10–11	91
4:10	90
4:11	42, 88, 90
4:12–20	24, 30, 88, 91–95
4:12	34, 42, 78, 91, 92
4:13–15	34
4:13	92
4:14	93
4:15–16	42, 88
4:15	93
4:16	93
4:17–18	94
4:17	44, 94
4:18	94

SCRIPTURE INDEX

Reference	Pages
4:19	34, 42, 94, 105, 117, 125
4:20	42, 88, 94, 95
4:21–31	24, 59, 89, 95–98, 102, 103
4:21	33, 42, 88, 96
4:22–23	96
4:23	98
4:24–26	97
4:25	127
4:26	106, 127
4:28	34, 42, 97, 98, 127
4:29	98
4:30	98
4:31	34, 42, 98, 106
5:1—6:10	21, 22, 24, 99–120
5:1–26	117
5:1–15	24, 30, 91, 101–9
5:1	59, 91, 100, 103, 106, 107, 108, 110, 111, 123
5:2–6	103
5:2–4	42, 100
5:2–3	124
5:2	58, 103, 114
5:3	58, 103, 108
5:4	33, 41, 42, 104
5:5–6	100
5:5	104, 106, 109, 118, 119, 120, 125
5:6	58, 104, 105, 106, 106, 120, 125
5:7–12	31, 100, 107
5:7	42, 44, 57, 71, 105, 106, 119
5:8–12	42
5:8–9	118
5:8	44, 106
5:9	106
5:10	44, 106
5:11–12	107
5:11	31, 34, 42, 58, 106, 107, 124, 125, 127
5:12	44, 107
5:13—6:10	108
5:13–25	108
5:13–15	100
5:13–14	111, 117
5:13	34, 42, 59, 107, 108, 111, 116
5:14	108, 116
5:15	109, 110, 116, 118, 119
5:16—6:10	42, 98, 105, 109, 125
5:16–26	24, 36, 109–14, 115, 116, 118, 119
5:16–17	108
5:16	91, 100, 103, 110, 111, 113, 114, 116, 118, 120
5:17–18	113
5:17	108, 111, 119
5:18–23	113
5:18	112, 116, 118, 120
5:19–23	113, 116
5:19–21	112
5:21	112, 118
5:22–23	112, 118
5:22	105, 108, 113
5:23	113, 116
5:24	113, 126
5:25	114, 116, 118, 120, 127
5:26	108, 114, 116, 118, 119
6:1–10	24, 110, 115–20
6:1–5	118
6:1–2	117
6:1	34, 42, 116, 117, 118, 119
6:2	108, 116, 117
6:3–5	117
6:3–4	117
6:5	118
6:6–10	118
6:6	118, 119
6:7–8	118
6:7	118
6:8	119
6:9	119
6:10	91, 119, 123
6:11–18	21, 24, 42, 121–28
6:11–17	24, 122–27
6:11	123
6:12–17	31
6:12–13	44, 127

Galatians (continued)

6:12	58, 59, 94, 124, 125
6:13	58, 94, 124, 125
6:14–15	31, 126
6:14	31, 36, 125, 126
6:15	36, 58, 125, 127
6:16	126, 127
6:17	31, 127
6:18	24, 34, 42, 128

Ephesians

1:1	27
1:2	34
5:5	112
6:24	128

Philippians

1:1	31
1:2	34
1:8	54
2:16	57
3:6	51
4:21–22	122
4:21	122
4:23	128

Colossians

1:1	27, 31
1:2	34
4:10–14	122
4:15	122
4:18	123, 128

Philemon

1:1	31
1:3	34
1:19	123
1:23–24	122
1:25	128

1 Thessalonians

1:1	31, 34
5:26	122
5:28	128

2 Thessalonians

1:1	31
1:2	34
3:17	123
3:18	128

1 Timothy

1:2	34
1:13	51
2:7	54
6:21	128

2 Timothy

1:1	27
1:2	34
4:19	122
4:21	122
4:22	128

Titus

1:4	34
3:15	122, 128

Hebrews

9:16	78

www.ingramcontent.com/pod-product-compliance
Lightning Source LLC
Chambersburg PA
CBHW070302230426
43664CB00014B/2610